Invisib

Invisible Servant

Richard Welch

Authentic

11 10 09 08 07 06 05   7 6 5 4 3 2 1

First published 2005 by Authentic Media,
9 Holdom Avenue, Bletchley, Milton Keynes, Bucks,
MK1 1QR, UK and
PO Box 1047, Waynesboro, GA 30830-2047, USA.

British Library Cataloguing in Publication Data
A catalogue record for this book is available from the British
Library

1-86024-532-3

Cover design by www.jaffadesign.uk.com
Print Management by Adare Carwin
Printed in Great Britain by Haynes, Sparkford, Yeovil,
Somerset

This book is dedicated to the
people of Albania.

To Ian,

It's been great to meet you
and I wish you well on your
own journey of faith.

Warm regards,

Richard

'Patient endurance attaineth to all
things...'

St. Teresa of Avila.

CONTENTS

SPECIAL THANKS

I would like to thank my lovely wife Linda for her commitment in helping me put this book together. Her natural aptitude for editing, as she sat at our Saranda kitchen table faithfully typing on a laptop every word, including numerous drafts, has been invaluable. Regular power cuts, as well as umpteen breaks to eat cake and make cups of tea, were all taken in her stride.

My thanks also go to David Waite, a man who has become my close friend and agent. His expert eye and cutting wit has made the experience of writing all the richer.

Finally, I am indebted to many, many people for sticking with me throughout the period spanned by this book. You know who you are, and I express my sincere gratitude to you.

Richard Welch

FOREWORD

Albania. The only country in the world officially declared to be fully atheistic. No place for God, his children, the Church or the Bible. I don't know how many times my Open Doors colleagues and I have told this to people in our Open Doors meetings. We did this to challenge Christians to pray for this closed country, and what looked like an impossible situation. For years we organized prayer tours 'to bring down the walls'.

Then suddenly it happened; the doors opened. The impossible became possible. The forbidden Word of God became freely available. I had the privilege to hand over the first copy of the new Albanian Bible to the President who was a Muslim. Evangelistic meetings began to take place.

Albania had changed because God's people prayed. For God nothing is impossible (Lk. 1:37). May this book challenge you to trust God and never give up.

Brother Andrew
Open Doors

INTRODUCTION

When Richard Welch and I became friends, little did I know that one day I would be relaying messages to him from the British SAS. This book describes how an every-day man received a remarkable call on his life. Through making selfless choices and denying selfish ambitions, Richard discovered that life can become more colourful and purposeful. There are many causes worth living for, but few worth dying for.

It was in the summer of 1994 when I first met Richard: a tall, athletic and unassuming man. His warmth and genuineness was evident as soon as we spoke. As time passed, his concise questions and willingness to help the Albanian people in desperate need impressed me.

In making probably the most important choice of his life, he embarked upon an adventure that would place him totally in God's hands. Many of the certainties of life were replaced by uncertainties, as Richard left behind a secure job, a reliable health service and the comforts of home, family and friends. He even left Wolverhampton Wanderers, his beloved football team behind!

As a leader of a mission-fired church it had always been my dream to see people of all ages and back-grounds make a positive difference in lands they never dreamed they would visit. Richard tells his story with humour and dignity, understating the many challenges that faced him. I admire him greatly because he is a man who didn't just talk his dream; he decided to walk it with all its impossibilities. His faith was put to the test when he left the comfort of the church pew to go to a place where bullets would fly around his head.

If you read this book with an open heart and mind, you can't help but be moved by this compelling story of one man's life. To give love and show kindness, he had to break down the barriers of suspicion and mistrust. Many of us give up at the first sign of rejection. Richard persisted and broke through, a lesson to each of us who choose to be givers in life.

I thank Richard for his honesty and openness, and especially for his friendship. Richard has helped me to see how God uses ordinary people to do extraordinary things.

Thank you, Richard, for sharing your story.

Gary Spicer, Senior Pastor
King's Community Church, Bedworth

Our vision is:
To bring the positive message of the Christian faith
through faith and example,
with the aim of touching the Albanian people
emotionally, physically, educationally and spiritually.
To raise a standard that is sensitive to the culture,
but will add to the quality of their lives,
in order to build their self-esteem.

King's Community Church, Bedworth

SPY IN THE CAMP?

It was noisy and dark inside the Chinook helicopter. As I remained sitting in the Land Rover that minutes earlier had transported me from Borsh, Southern Albania, to a dramatic pick-up a few miles further along the rocky shoreline, it barely seemed real. The vehicle only came to a halt after being driven inside the belly of the helicopter. SAS soldiers were all around me, by now swigging from bottles of water, my few belongings packed into a rucksack placed between my feet. My home for the past eighteen months was now considered too dangerous to live in. 'We're taking you to Italy,' the front passenger of the Land Rover shouted into my left ear, as he turned to address me. By now we were airborne.

* * *

Albania was sliding into anarchy, following the collapse of pyramid savings schemes. A million guns had been looted by a people who were demanding recompense for their losses. Hardship was no stranger to Albania. The helicopter's initial touchdown point, just across the water from Corfu, was only yards away from a castle built by one of Albania's more colourful historical figures. Ali Pasha Tepelena fought against the Ottoman Turks during the twilight of their 400-year occupation of his country. Within seconds of take-off, we were flying over the site of what was once a top-secret submarine base. Now, in 1997, it was a decaying relic of the former 'People's Socialist Republic of Albania'. The road on which gunmen had stopped us minutes earlier had formerly been out of bounds for decades to all non-military personnel. It was lined with some of the seven hundred thousand concrete bunkers that had been constructed in a five-year period, part of a national fortification programme. 'I've never seen anything like this before,' said the SAS man in the front passenger seat. At a time when other Eastern European states underwent de-Stalinisation, Albania had remained hard line. Every one of its citizens was given compulsory military training in preparation for the coming onslaught of enemy invasion, as predicted by their paranoid dictators. The tiny Balkan state had entered an era of self-imposed political, economic and cultural isolation. Poverty, mass internment, forced labour camps, secret police informers and official state atheism made recent history bleak. It wasn't until December 1990 that the authorities dismantled Stalin's statue in Tirana, Albania's capital city. The following year, the Communist government resigned and a multi-party government was formed, the first in forty-seven years.

* * *

As our helicopter lurched up and down, closely following the contours of the mountainous terrain just a few feet below, I had time to reflect on what I was leaving behind. A British television interviewer was to later introduce me onto his programme as, 'A man who was airlifted from one of the most dangerous places in the world.' In fact, the day of my departure could not have begun more quietly. I'd gone for a jog, breakfasted at a neighbour's home, even had time to call and say good-bye to some of the village children. The paradox of the situation wasn't lost on me. Despite a wretched history and a full-scale crisis on its hands, I left Albania with a smile.

'See you when you get back,' were my neighbour's parting words.

* * *

Going to visit Albania, let alone going to live there, hadn't been something I'd ever envisaged doing. I was 37 years old and working as a middle manager in what used to be called The Department of Health and Social Security. Although I didn't really think that being a civil servant would yield professional fulfilment, after seventeen years I was on an even keel and wasn't looking to move on. I'd divorced four years earlier and was living alone in a small house with a friendly feel to it in the countryside. I belonged to a small, closely knit family and I was fortunate enough to have a great circle of friends. Getting divorced had been the most radical episode in life to date. As a boy, together with my younger brother Vin, I enjoyed my home life very much. The most daring thing we'd get up to would be letting car tyres down. We targeted the pub-goers who parked their cars at the top of the long driveway to our house, thereby making it inaccessible to us. On heady nights we'd telephone 'Dial-a-Disc', when Mom and Dad were out, to hear such classics as 'Johnny Reggae' sung by The Piglets.

My father, Raymond, was a Congregational Church minister and we loved him very much. He had a boyish sense of humour and we were devastated when he died suddenly of a heart attack whilst working in the garden. My brother and I were 14 and 15 years old respectively. As youngsters, we'd sometimes be asked if we wanted to follow dad's footsteps into the ministry. We'd say shyly that we didn't think so and never considered it seriously as we entered adulthood. Mom got re-married, to Doug, a friend from childhood, and moved to Leeds. Many years later, brother Vin married Bev and bought a home just a stone's throw from our old family home in Upper Gornal, Dudley, West Midlands.

With the exception of a four-year period when I readily admit I lost my way in life, church involvement had been one of the important facets of my life. At that time I was attending Himley Road Methodist Church in God's own country, Gornal. Looking back, although I was a believer, I had never really walked the narrow path. Life had become comfortable with many of the world's traditional securities in place, such as a house, car and a good steady salary.

Big doors swing on small hinges. Whether I actually attended the charity event I'd purchased a ticket for, a fundraiser for Albanian aid, was of little consequence, I thought. On a summer's evening during 1994, the M6 did its best to hold on to me for as long as possible, as I made my way home from work in Birmingham. I was feeling tired, so it was tempting to simply go home instead, knowing that I'd done my bit by purchasing a ticket. In the end, I decided to attend and quietly slipped into the church hall in Kingswinford, Dudley, taking a seat towards the back.

The guest speaker was Bill Hamilton, a BBC reporter who'd travelled to Albania with the England football team, to cover a World Cup qualifying game in March 1989. Despite his professional interest, he made little comment about the game. His heart had been captured

by the Albanian people, who had suffered much deprivation during almost half a century of extreme communism. He had witnessed great hardships during his visit.
I was so moved by what I heard that I remarked to Steve
Jones, the friend who'd sold me the ticket, that if there
was something I could do to help I'd like to do it. 'Well,
my brother-in-law, Gary Spicer, is the pastor of a church
in Bedworth, near Coventry, and he sends groups of volunteers over to Albania on short term visits to help out,'
he said.

* * *

One October evening later that year, I found myself sitting in the departure lounge of Birmingham Airport,
along with eight other volunteers, about to depart on a
flight to Corfu. We were to meet up with a missionary
couple, Theo and Sandra Goutzios, who were skippering
a boat called *Morning Star*. From there we would sail
down the sixteen-mile strip of the Ionian Sea that sepa-
rates Corfu from Southern Albania. Upon arrival, we
would drop anchor in the port of Saranda and *Morning
Star* would be our home for the next twelve days. I
wasn't an experienced traveller, so the prospect of getting a glimpse of Greece as well as Albania added to the
excitement that lay ahead. We'd met together as a group
a couple of times at what was then called Bedworth
Christian Centre, later to become King's Community
Church. This had helped us to get to know each other a
little by the time our departure date arrived; I liked the
fact that we were a team of people with mixed life experiences. Richard Blower, a stocky man in his forties, was
a former coalminer and led the team, together with his
wife Olwyn.

As we sailed towards Saranda the following day, Gary
Spicer, with us for a few days at the start of our short

stint, sat on deck and told us that what lay ahead would probably challenge us all. Gary first visited Albania as a day-tripper from Corfu, a couple of years earlier and so began the Bedworth involvement. On this trip we would be helping to patch up and paint the town's maternity hospital, among other things. It contained a crude abortion clinic and we were told that some women had numerous terminations in the most brutal of circumstances. Our manner, as we teamed up with full-time church aid workers based in Saranda, should be co-operative and sensitive. As our boat pulled into port, we saw the imposing bank of drab, unimaginative concrete apartment blocks that almost reached down to the water's edge. Just as Theo had predicted, umpteen port policemen piled on board to examine our passports and receive entry payments. Theo was determined not to pay above the prescribed rate and firmly resisted any attempts to extricate more US dollars from us. All of us shook hands with all of them before and after a half-hour interlude of reading, re-reading and the eventual stamping of our passports. Before finally disembarking, they cheerfully assured us that everything would be alright. During the course of our stay we suspected that some of the very same policemen sneaked on board one night, because the following morning all of our shoes were missing.

During those twelve days I saw and experienced things that made deep impressions on me. However, despite my feelings of compassion and intrigue, there was no irresistible impulse to make my home there. In fact, the opposite was true; I thought several times to myself, *'Wouldn't it be a nightmare to be living in a place like this?'*

We were briefly having our eyes opened to the lives of people living in austerity. Our walk through the town gave us something of an insight into the people's living conditions. We couldn't help but notice the very poor state of repair the roads and pavements were in, as we constantly avoided gaping holes along the way. It seemed that every water pipe one's eyes fell upon was leaking heavily. There were several roadside corrugated iron kiosks in view, out of which limited grocery supplies and poor quality fruit and vegetables were sold. Occasionally, we'd come across a side road that had a steady trickle of foul-smelling untreated sewage running down its rocky surface.

We were able to do superficial, cosmetic repairs to the maternity hospital, which had a sign on its main doorway warning of the danger of cholera. The husbands of the patients were not allowed through its battered doors, so we felt even more conspicuous because we foreigners were allowed where the local men were not. There was little evidence of medical supplies or drugs inside. We all heaved when the meal trolley passed by, containing an unappetizing-looking stew. No doubt women's screams are common to maternity hospitals all over the world. Particularly disturbing here was the sight of aborted foetuses, lying around in plastic buckets near the entrance to the ugly and stark abortion room.

One day several tins of paint disappeared. The hospital official on hand didn't speak English, but Richard's gestures left no room for ambiguity; unless they were recovered, we wouldn't continue. Blank expressions were accompanied by lots of shoulder shrugging, but after a while the tins miraculously reappeared and work resumed.

Painting the home of a lady without hearing or speech was really enjoyable, as was an impromptu game of football at the orphanage, when we were given permission to call in and say, 'Hello'.

There were welcome moments of lightness. Our daily wash involved soaping ourselves up, before jumping off deck into the clear blue sea below. Sandra always sent us off to work on a good breakfast; pancakes with chocolate spread were a particular favourite.

As we sailed back towards Greece, to begin our homeward journey, I had many things to think about. I thought about a conversation with Theo and Sandra, during which I'd asked them what the likes of an institutionalized civil servant could possibly do in a place like Albania, if called upon to live there. My question had been prompted by a disturbing thought that lay within me, *'What if Jesus Christ called me to follow him to Albania today, just as he'd called his disciples to follow him when he walked the earth two thousand years earlier?'* It was a question I didn't really want to answer. Theo and Sandra said that the content of a person's heart was of primary importance. Skill levels were of little value if our attitude prohibits God's hand from moving freely. If our hearts are open and willing, he can use us power-fully, way beyond our expectations.

As I sat on deck, together with fellow Black Country-man and bunk mate Brian Evans, an industrial chemist, for a moment contemplating nothing more important than whether I fancied a cup of coffee or not, a truly special thing happened. Some dolphins swam alongside the boat as it cut its way through the shimmering sea. They were in a playful mood, effortlessly swapping port and starboard sides of our vessel. Several times they briefly reared up out of the water as if they were putting on a bit of a show. A voice within me spoke with great clarity, *'If you remain in my will you will be as free as they are.'* I was taken aback but said nothing of the experience to my team-mates at the time. I hadn't ever experienced anything of this kind before and it gave me even more to think about.

* * *

After being back home for a few weeks, I made an appointment to see Gary Spicer. I found Gary to be a man outside of the usual mould of church leaders I had experienced. His radical vision for the church, combined with a lively sense of fun, made him a cross between Billy Graham and Del Boy from the TV series, *Only Fools and Horses.*

'I've come to tell you that Albania remains in my mind,' I said to him as we sat in his church office.

It wasn't a case of my feeling haunted or troubled by what I'd experienced on my short trip, it was more a case of a persistent feeling that I had to go and talk to him. To be frank, part of me wanted to simply be 'released' by him, and to be told that there was nothing more for me to do. Then I would be able to carry on with my life much the same as before.

'That's interesting,' he said, 'we're looking for a full-time man on the ground over in Albania.'

My heart sank a little. Although Gary, to his credit, never made any attempt to persuade me that I was the man for the job, which was unsalaried, I had an inner conviction about it. Albania would be even less inviting in January, which meant that it would be a good time to further explore my feelings towards the place. Was I really being called there or not? I accordingly took more of my annual leave entitlement from work and reached for my passport once again.

* * *

Sure enough, Saranda was cold and damp when Gary and I arrived. We had three travelling companions, including Jeremy Parkes, a church pastor from Netherton in the heart of the Black Country. It was an eventful five days, but one incident in particular served as a signpost to me as I considered further my personal path ahead. We were introduced to a man called Skënder, the town's Ear, Nose and Throat specialist. He gave us all a tour of the spartan General Hospital and then invited us back to his home for coffee. Just a few minutes' walk away from the hospital, we were soon walking up the three flights of concrete steps of an unlit stairwell that led to Skënder's apartment.

'Home,' said our host, as his eyes twinkled beneath a set of bushy eyebrows.

His wife Liri welcomed us all in and we were relieved that she too spoke quite good English. I removed my boots in their tiled hallway and Skënder gave me his slippers to wear. After a few moments, I asked if I could wash my hands and headed for their bathroom. No water came out of the taps, but Skënder, anticipating my need, walked into the bathroom holding a pitcher of clean water.

'Here we are, I'll help you,' he said humbly, and proceeded to pour water over my hands until the soap had done its job.

It seemed that the locals were accustomed to long periods without running water or electricity each day. Without comment, he handed me a towel and left the room. I was deeply moved by his action, which taught me a lesson about serving others. Skënder later recounted a boyhood recollection of his mother washing the feet of guests who came to their home. His memory triggered a thought within me about Jesus washing the feet of his disciples. Being briefly immersed in a culture that had at one time observed the custom somehow made the biblical account all the more imaginable.

As we were leaving Skënder's home that evening, he took me by the arm. We walked past a cow, munching its way through a huge pile of household garbage strewn across some open ground.

'Well, Reechard, what do you think of my country?' he asked me.

A watery sunset was partially in view through the spaces between the grey apartment blocks. I said something about nature being beautiful.

With a wry grin, he said, 'Aah, what God has made is very beautiful, but what man has made is very ugly.'

* * *

Back home, the leadership team at church gave me thirty days to make my decision. My colleagues at work were following my progress with interest. When I talked to my senior managers about the crossroads I was at, I couldn't have asked for more support from them. Janet, my immediate line manager, a committed Christian, even spoke about how she felt positively challenged by my stance in considering such a personal change of direction. Two close friends suggested that I could be about to ruin my life if I went to live in Albania, another was less circumspect and simply said, 'You must be bonkers!' Most of my family, friends and associates were part horrified, part curious. They wisely resisted offering advice, it was a decision only I could make. Mom and Doug very sensitively explored the possibility that I may have been weighed down a little by guilt hanging around from getting divorced. However, I was quite sure that if I did go to Albania it wouldn't be as a form of penance for the previous wrong turnings I'd made in life. It was a fair question to ask, but guilt wasn't a motive. Although I felt daunted by the potential challenges that lay ahead, the whole experience to date had been a very positive one. I realized that the practicalities of going to live in such an alien environment; struggling with the language, coping with less than appealing food and making ends meet, were not in fact the main challenges. The underlying question was a fundamental one. Did I truly believe in God and, if so, did I honestly trust him with my life?

St Paul had written, a little under two thousand years ago, about God's will being 'good, pleasing and perfect'. In truth, I'd never unreservedly sought his will for my life before. I realized that if I was not to miss something important, I had to position myself accordingly. What was the point in earnestly seeking direction if I wasn't prepared to act upon it, should I be required to make a move? I had to unclutter my mind of the negative 'ifs', 'buts' and 'maybes'. No doubt many of you will be familiar with the following words of C.S. Lewis. I found that he crystallized much of what was going through my mind at that time. 'Christianity is a statement, which, if false, is of no importance. If it is true, it is of infinite importance. The one thing it cannot be is of moderate importance.'[1]

I came to the conclusion that the creator of the universe was more important than my leather armchair and my new CD player. That may sound trite, but the truth had been that treasured possessions had, up until then, created a formidable barrier to 'fixing my eyes on what is unseen'. I didn't follow up that personal revelation by purging my home of every nick-nack in sight, but I did try to see things through a changed perspective.

My experience was that once I turned that particular corner, answers to my prayers for 'clear direction' became increasingly obvious. It seemed that almost everywhere I looked there were road signs saying, 'Albania this way'.

A talk given by Ian Green, one of the leaders of the church at Bedworth, helped me further. He related a survey that had been carried out amongst fifty people aged 95 years old and above. They were asked the question, 'If you could live your life over again, what would you do differently?' One of the three most common answers was, 'I'd take more risks.' As a civil servant, the relatively high degree of job security had the potential to dampen any ambition to step into the unknown. In addition, I am conservative by nature, so I found the story challenging.

In a completely unrelated short visit I made to America, about three or four months after my first trip to Albania, I was staggered by something a woman said to me outside The Obelisk in Washington DC. I'd asked if she minded taking my photograph and we engaged in conversation as she handed the camera back to me. She picked up on me being English and said that although she'd never visited England, her husband, a US serviceman, had worked in Albania. She went on to say that even though we didn't know each other, she felt compelled to encourage me to make my home in Albania! I shouldn't worry about anything, finances included. I am convinced that she was a genuine message bearer. What she had told me just wasn't the sort of thing strangers normally say to each other.

I was absolutely sure that I was doing the right thing when I resigned from my job in July 1995 and announced that I would be emigrating to what was the poorest country in Europe. My work colleagues reacted to the news with remarkable generosity. The personnel from the two office sites set about doing whatever they could to send me off with a financial gift to help meet my expenses, once I was on the ground.

* * *

Just a month later, I stepped off the ferry in Saranda with two suitcases containing my belongings. An avaricious port policewoman asked me to open my bags. Several audiocassettes spilt out onto the ground and she gestured to take one for herself. I thought to myself, 'Not flippin' likely, mate!' but settled instead for a smile and a polite, 'No, I'm sorry.'

I lived in Saranda for two months, renting a two-bedroom ground floor flat from a woman called Athena. Every so often she would come in unannounced, look around, straighten the cover on the ancient wooden framed settee and then wander out again.

Dutch missionaries showed me great kindness during that time. Not only was I regularly welcomed into their homes, where I enjoyed good coffee and home-made cakes, they helped equip me with some essential household supplies. They were relatively well resourced and produced an electric cooker, as well as six sets of bunk-beds from a warehouse they rented just out of town. These provisions were extremely valuable, because such items were not available in Saranda. The property I was renting was only modestly equipped and with the imminent arrival of teams, I had little time to establish myself.

Two weeks after moving to Albania, the first of three teams, comprised of people from Bedworth and her partner churches, arrived. With the onset of those visits came another challenge – communal living. I had previously enjoyed my own space at home, back in England, so working, eating and sleeping alongside others took a little getting used to. Hosting teams was to become a regular feature of spring and summer for many years to come. A typical team, made up of eight people, would arrive with their bags laden with goodies to help them, and me, through their stay. In addition to bringing their own bedding, biscuits, chocolate, powdered milk, tea bags and tinned meats were always popular. Very few foodstuffs were available 'on the ground'.

When it came to putting a programme of work together, my Dutch friends, Jasper and Andre, were again helpful. There was no shortage of practical work to be done
in the town, as most public buildings were in a shocking
state of repair. We also looked for ways of supporting
Solon, a young Greek pastor, who, together with his wife
Pia, had boldly gone to live in Saranda almost as soon as
the old regime fell from power.

I was grateful for the moments of humour my guests
brought with them. One night, all residents living within a quarter-mile radius of where we were staying, must
have been woken up by the chilling sound of women's
screams. My female guests, already feeling victimized by
the local mosquito population, finally snapped when
two or three of them spotted some of the creepy crawlies
they were sharing their bedroom with. Another team,
from Cleveland, Ohio, had the job of helping repair the
town's prison. In return for our labours, we were given
one hour to talk to the prisoners, with the aid of a translator, about our Christian faith. One day, the American's
pastor, Randy, took a large swig from a bottle of paint
thinner he'd mistaken for water. We joked with him the
next morning about the patch of ceiling above where
he'd slept; due to the fumes on his breath, all the paint
had peeled off!

Some solid and enduring friendships have been
forged with people I first welcomed as strangers when
they came to stay with me. I usually felt deflated when
guests departed, but also relieved when things had gone
well during their stay. In a land of so many unknown
quantities, I felt a heavy burden of responsibility for the
wellbeing of my friends.

With the arrival of winter, the time came to leave
Saranda and move to Borsh, 45 kilometres up the coast.
My heart felt very heavy. I'd made some friends in

Saranda and was getting to find my way around without having to go everywhere with a big ball of string under my arm. The first time I was driven along the twisting and narrow route from Saranda, I gasped as Borsh suddenly came into view. After turning yet another corner, on a road that clung to the side of one mountain after another, I found myself looking down over a huge plain. Some fifty years earlier, a Workers' Co-operative Farm had been set up. Hundreds of olive and citrus trees were planted, creating work for the dozens of men and women who were imported from other parts of the country. The immigrants were housed in a purpose-built neighbourhood called 'Ferme' meaning 'farm'. I was to find out that decades later, they were still considered to be 'outsiders' by the other villagers. The geography of the location made it spectacularly beautiful. Three sides of the plain were bordered by imposing mountains, in whose shadows little pockets of housing nestled. The other boundary was provided by a dramatic sweep of coastline. A beach of white pebbles separated the orchard from a clear sea of jade and blue.

In preparation for taking up residency there, I made several exploratory visits by taxi. I was to pioneer a work in a place where, according to living memory, no other Western Europeans had previously lived. Although I had a say in it, the church leadership team at Bedworth had the last word in deciding the location. It suited me that way because I would have felt uncomfortable making the personal decision to live in such an attractive place. Although the isolation factor was considerable and life in Borsh would lack creature comforts, other people lived in much more hostile environments. We all sensed that Borsh was simply 'the right place', even though there was little foundation to build on. Pioneering work meant that, at times, I would inevitably feel I was living in a far-flung wilderness. I had no idea what lay ahead, but on my side was the unshakable belief that I was where I was meant to be. I'd never before prayed about anything with such a hunger for direction.

My initial visit to Borsh had been made in the company of Dr Skënder. He knew many of its residents because he had once practised medicine in the area. Skënder introduced me to a man called Lavdosh, somebody I always seemed to bump into during subsequent visits to the village. Lavdosh was 52 years old and had a wife called Kosta. They had four daughters, one of whom was married and living in Athens. Also included in the extended family circle was their cow, an important accessory to village life. Lavdosh had a wiry frame, a generous nose and a fine head of curly hair. By contrast, Kosta's hair was thick and straight. She looked accustomed to hard physical work and the feel of her skin confirmed this as we shook hands. My need for a place to live and Lavdosh's opportunism, combined with an attitude of, 'Any friend of Skënder is a friend of mine,' were the contributory factors in me being offered accommodation in his home.

For the handsome payment of $100 a month, I received full board and lodging. They lived in the Ferme neighbourhood, a square grid of mainly single-storey constructions, built from the cheapest available material – concrete. A network of pathways, that were only wide enough for one person, connected the dozen or so rows of dwellings. At some point along most of the high boundary walls, the residents had suspended plastic dolls or goats' horns. This was an act of superstition to ward off evil spirits. The resident ducks evidently appreciated their muddy habitat by the noises they made as they waddled about the place.

Lavdosh's single-storey home had two bedrooms and a bathroom comprising a Turkish toilet and cold water tap. The stone-floored lounge was divided from a minute cooking area by a piece of curtain. In the grounds of their modest garden, vines grew overhead. A neatly stacked pile of wood provided fuel for heating the water used for the weekly clothes wash in their yard. There was also a shop/bar, which stood alone inside the confines of the high garden walls, capped with pieces of broken glass cemented into place. The shop sold only basic food supplies such as pasta, rice, plain biscuits and fizzy drinks.

The family showed me kindness, despite not being able to speak English and my Albanian still not being good. We communicated by smiles and sign language. Mealtimes were difficult at first. I didn't look forward to them but found that I was gradually able to get through them with decreasing degrees of discomfort. In a typical day, I would eat an apple, honey or figs with bread for breakfast, with a further meal in the late afternoon. Something that took some getting used to was the practice of cooking the day's food in the late morning and eating it several hours later, by which time it was of course cold. The meal might have been a type of soup with a generous helping of locally produced olive oil. This would invariably be accompanied by a dish of onions, olives and oranges sliced up and well lubricated in olive oil, together with bread and very fatty meat. If I was faced with something unpalatable, I was usually able to surreptitiously remove it, wrapped in a tissue. This wasn't possible with soup, of course, so I just had to get used to eating it. Much of the food was home-grown and it was in plentiful supply.

During mealtimes, it wasn't uncommon for Lavdosh to come running in from the bar, pick up a plate of food from the family's meal table, and take it to a hungry customer.

Occasionally, I strayed into the bar in the evenings. This was an exclusively male domain. Men sat around the nine or ten tables inside, smoking inexpensive cigarettes, 'contrabanda', and drinking *raki*. Arguments about politics and money were usually on offer too. One night, a man called Razip was in there with his brothers. He was a fearsome looking man, in his mid-thirties I'd guess, with a thick beard and long, shaggy hair. *'Maybe John the Baptist used to look like Razip,'* I thought to myself, as he'd noisily try to get my attention. After a few minutes, my eyes returned to his. He'd soaked one of his fingers in *raki* and then set fire to it with a cigarette lighter. Holding it aloft, his brothers joined him in looking in my direction, partly giving an unspoken endorsement to his act of bravado, but also searching my face for a reaction. I gave him a nervous, watery smile and took another sip of my cola, whilst trying to look tough.

Back inside the family lounge, the nightly entertainment was underway. In front of a grainy black and white television set, Kosta, Lavdosh's quietly accommodating wife, sat down with her daughters to watch a Greek soap opera. *Lampsee* wasn't subtitled into Albanian, so it fell to Lumi, a 20-year-old teacher at the nearby infant school, to translate the proceedings. It was a wonderful spectacle to observe. Everyone sat in complete silence, all eyes transfixed on the screen. If anyone spoke the others would give a loud, 'Shush!' When the inevitable commercial break came along, Lumi sprang into action, translating the previous ten minutes' worth of dialogue into Albanian inside two minutes. Questions would be put to her, but if they spilled over into the restart of the programme, the questioner would be drowned by more shushes. In the event of the picture fading, it was the job of Dori, the rebellious teenager, to clamber up on to the roof, via a window grille, to readjust the position of the television aerial.

After the excitement of *Lampsee*, the pace of the average evening slowed down. I'd sometimes reach for my Albanian grammar book, but usually ended up helping Lumi with her English instead.

I hadn't taken enough warm clothing with me, so would get really cold in the evenings. My feet, knees, fingers and nose would slowly go numb and I would look forward to going to bed. Stone floors, loose rugs, and inefficient one-bar electric heaters were the norm. Central heating and fitted carpets were yet to arrive in that part of the world. I thought that retiring anytime after 8 p.m. was acceptable. Anything earlier may have been considered both rude and antisocial; hurting the feelings of my hosts wasn't something I wanted to risk doing. On going to the bedroom, I placed my clothes over the chair before clambering into my sleeping bag, which lay on an old metal-framed bed. After about half an hour, my feet would thaw out. As I lay there, I enjoyed listening to music on the personal stereo my former colleagues had bought me as a leaving gift. I welcomed the sanctuary of my own private domain. Outside was an unfamiliar world, but here, I was alone with my thoughts, in a dark, warm place where I did not have to be 'on duty' in an alien environment. The faces and voices of my family and friends came into mind and I was immune from outside intrusion. For these reasons, bedtime was the best moment of the day.

After a few weeks, a new chest freezer appeared in the shop. No doubt this had been purchased out of the handsome income my board money was providing for Lavdosh. He was not initially persuaded by my suggestion, no doubt completely incomprehensible to him that, once switched on, it should be left running. He opted instead to, as he saw it, save electricity by switching it off last thing every night. When I went to mop up the inevitable pool of water next morning, he looked horrified. 'That's women's work,' he said, and then smiled at the curious spectacle of a man holding a mop.

To begin the process of easing my way into a tough, often inscrutable community, I sensed that patience, sensitivity and determination were required of me. Why should the villagers simply assume that my reasons for being amongst them were not born out of subversion or sinister personal gain? For decades, their political leaders had instructed them to view all westerners as prospective spies. Even though the regime's lifespan had now expired, it would have been unreasonable of me to expect anything other than a cautious reception, at best. Furthermore, friends in Saranda had warned me to be careful in Borsh. 'They're a strange lot,' was the gist of the comments made by their compatriots. I decided that quiet, low-key stints in the nearby orchards, to help Lavdosh's family pick olives, would put me into the public's watchful eye without fuelling its suspicions about me. I was determined to make a positive impact, but felt that extravagant gestures to help ingratiate myself with the villagers would set our work off on a bad footing.

Getting the olives off the trees and into the dealers' lorries was hard work and my soft bureaucrat's hands quickly blistered. Olive growing, like all other enterprises, used to be an exclusively State managed operation. Nowadays, it was a matter between families, who appeared to have come to an understanding over who picked what. The village women showed remarkable strength, carrying sacks of 60lb/30kg on their backs out of the orchard at the end of the working day. Climbing trees and hacking away branches with axes seemed to come as naturally to them as making butter or washing their family's clothes in streams of cold water. If it rained hard, olive picking would be cancelled for the day. On one such day, I accompanied Lumi to the infant school where she taught, just a few yards from their home. The single-storey stone building had several windows smashed in its two classrooms. All the children spontaneously jumped to their feet when I walked in; they were generally very polite towards me in and out of school. Many would reach up to kiss me after becoming accustomed to regularly seeing me walking around their neighbourhood. As the rain poured outside, I marvelled at how, on Lumi's instruction, several of the children moved their old-fashioned desks with built-in benches, to a spot where the rain couldn't drip on them from the holes in the old tiled roof. It was done in such a matter-of-fact way that it was obviously a routine manoeuvre for them.

As the weeks became months, the regular rhythm of village life stirred only occasionally. Blood on the step of Lavdosh's shop one day was the consequence of a knife fight the previous evening, but little mention was made of it. On a different occasion, a lot of shouting was to be heard near to where I was staying. I peered around the gate to see numerous people, young and old, arguing passionately between themselves. It transpired that a locally appointed five-man commission, set up to deliberate on the vexed question of previously State owned land being allocated to private ownership, had published it's initial findings. Clearly, that process was to be a bitterly contested one. Of less magnitude was the rare sight of carrots for sale in Lavdosh's shop one morning on his return from a visit to Tirana. That sent many of the women scurrying back home for their purses, to quickly snap up what would provide a welcome change on the meal table.

Of greater consequence to me personally was the unexpected arrival of a different kind in the shop. One evening, a local man came in and asked to speak to me. When I appeared, he greeted me in English!

'Hello, my name is Bashkim, I am the dentist,' he said.

These were the first words of my own language I'd heard from a village resident. We sat at a table as he told me that he'd secretly learnt English during the communist era. His eyes looked straight into mine from under his trilby, as he said he knew everybody in the village and would like to help me if I had any problems or needs. A nagging concern of mine was that I needed to find accommodation that would comfortably house the forthcoming visiting groups from England. Maybe he could help with that, but I chose not to mention it because there was something about him that I didn't feel sure about. Just two or three days later, Dori developed raging toothache. I volunteered to accompany her to Bashkim's house. Along the way we were given a wobbly ride on a passing motorbike by Afrim, a local electrician. Once inside the 'surgery', devoid of water or electricity, at the side of Bashkim's home, my toes curled up inside my boots at the sight of him setting about removing a nerve from one of her teeth without anaesthetic! He was still wearing his trilby at the end of the treatment when he asked us into his home for coffee. Again, he asserted his intention to help me integrate into the village. There was, however, a string attached to his offer. He would like me to meet the daughter of a friend of his, with a view to marrying her!

As that slightly embarrassing issue, for me at least, surfaced with tiresome regularity whenever our paths crossed, I decided to put a little distance between us. We remained on friendly terms, superficially at least, but I think I proved to be a disappointment to him, as his matchmaking aspirations came to nothing. Sterner challenges were lying ahead for me however, far beyond the range of Cupid's arrows or even the brutality of a dentist's chair.

---

[1]   C.S. Lewis, *Timeless at Heart* (London: Fount). Used with permission.

2

SHOULD I STAY OR SHOULD I GO?

Going to live in Albania had considerably broadened my horizons. Everything around me that I saw, heard or tasted was unfamiliar; the moon looked the same, but very little else. In other ways, the simplicity of village life gave the impression of my world being very small.

One night, as I sat in Lavdosh's lounge, I announced that I was going to catch a bus into Saranda the following morning. To be a little more precise, I used the words, 'Saranda, bus, tomorrow.' I may have pronounced them badly and even used them in the wrong order but, fortunately, my hosts understood what I was trying to say. They exchanged sideways glances, but despite feeling like a schoolboy who had just announced to his classmates that he was going to become an astronaut, I was set on a day's adventure.

Early the next morning, Lavdosh accompanied me to the place on the road where the aging single-decker bus would stop. He boarded with me, escorted me to a vacant seat, kissed me on both cheeks and said that the driver, a friend of his, would look after me. A strict no smoking policy was adhered to and some of the male passengers sucked on unlit cigarettes throughout the ninety-minute journey. Men sat alongside other men, but it was clear that mixed seating was to be avoided. From where I sat, I could keep my eyes on the road, through some of the holes in the floor of the bus. On this particular journey, I travelled part of the way alongside a chicken, with its head protruding out of a plastic carrier bag. On future expeditions, steel building rods were sometimes threaded down the centre isle. Another time, a three-piece suite was wired to the bus' roof. On reaching the owner's village, several male passengers were expected to clamber up on top, to help lower the furniture down to waiting hands. When a smarter new bus was purchased, the driver became more selective. A 'no food or livestock on board' policy was introduced and it was not uncommon for the bus to suddenly come to a halt, just a few minutes into the journey.

'Who's got fish in their shopping bag?' demanded the driver, who'd be standing by now, looking accusingly at his passengers. If no one owned up, his nostrils would lead him to the offending package, which would then be despatched to the luggage hold down below.

Upon my return home, on the day of my first bus adventure, I was carrying a prized possession. I had purchased a bunch of bananas from a man who was selling them from a box on a town pavement. It had been an enjoyable trip for other reasons too: my Dutch friends had been pleased to see me when I called in on them and I'd discovered a kiosk that sold Mars bars. In my early days, such a find was a rare treasure. In time, more and more familiar foods and household cleaning materials began to find their way onto Albanian shop shelves.

My search for rented accommodation, large enough to sleep a dozen people, was concluded when Lavdosh made a suggestion. In return for a sizeable payment of rent in advance, he would complete the building work on his future family home up in the mountainside neighbourhood of Hori. Groups of visitors from England would soon be on their way and up until then, I had nowhere to put them.

With my money in his pocket, Lavdosh hired an assortment of local men to finish the work. However, he hadn't bargained on their excessive wage demands. Thinking of the money that Lavdosh was making out of his rich English friend, they were jealous and wanted a share in the spoils. With patience and sensitivity, I may have been able to reach the village people, even build friendships. That said, I sensed that beneath it all there would be a persistent, 'Whatever he says and does is all very well, but he's not the same as we are,' attitude to contend with. Money may have the power to open some doors, but my perceived wealth created a formidable barrier to overcome. Coming from a rich country had a potentially pulverizing effect on my objectives. However, I had no complaints – it was *because* we had very different experiences of life that I was there. The house rental arrangement between Lavdosh and me afforded me some special privileges. Not only would I finance the work, I was expected to physically help with it too. So anxious was I to have the place ready, I helped dig the footings for a bathroom – a feature that was considered an unnecessary extravagance when I first requested it.

The new house was not ready in time for the arrival of my first group of guests – a carefully chosen group of craftsmen drafted in to finish the job. Lavdosh and his family moved out of their home to accommodate them. Up at the new property, a local electrician had pronounced it 'completed and ready to move into' in spite of the fact that one of the interior walls was later discovered to be carrying a live charge of 60 volts! The premises, which came to be known as our base house, comprised two bedrooms, a small kitchen, a bathroom, which sometimes had hot and cold running water, and a large lounge. This opened onto a balcony, which looked out across the orchard and then seawards.

Team visits apart, living alone in the modestly equipped base house gave me a welcome privacy. Somewhat ungraciously, my heart would sink if I heard a knock at my door in the evenings. The solitude was always a haven, never a prison. I spent little time at home during the day; I was keen to get to know both the people and the area.

Lavdosh's brother, Eqerem (an electrician), who lived next door, was a regular visitor in the evenings. He assumed that I would be lonely on my own, so would spend many hours sitting alongside me on the homemade whiteboard tool chest in my hallway. He became accustomed to drinking my Nescafé and asked many questions about things I'd brought from England with me. He envied my Swiss army knife even more than my spotted dressing gown. A little younger than Lavdosh, he loosely resembled his brother, but had a more ready sense of humour, which often became rather earthy.

Married to Zuli, like him a qualified electrician, they had two children of school age – Berti and Najda. Eqerem often invited me next door, where I'd always be well fed and watered whilst watching Albanian television news. His work was to operate the small hydroelectric plant. The village was the perfect setting, because a constant cascade of water rushed down from a mountain spring and flowed through its centre. The turbines inside the plant were a legacy of Albania's once close friendship with China. Eqerem somehow managed to keep the antiquated machinery in working order. He encouraged me to visit him regularly at his place of work. This was no more than a hundred square yards in size, with a small room attached to the side, where he had a bed and an old electric fire for cold winter nights. He often completed two consecutive eight-hour shifts, preferring that Zuli, who also worked there, stayed at home to look after the domestics. Sometimes the machinery would sparkle and crackle as Eqerem pulled various levers or turned handles to keep a modest flow of electricity running. At times, when it looked as though he couldn't resuscitate the cumbersome Chinese monsters, he would stand there looking at them questioningly as if he were appealing to their better nature.

I have little doubt that Eqerem, like his brother, saw me as a goose that laid golden eggs. However, I liked to believe that there was an element of genuine friendship between us, too. We often stood chatting near to his cherished beehives, situated a few yards from my home. He frequently told me:

'You are my only true friend in this village. Who else can I trust and talk to like you?'

Lavdosh's family continued to treat me with respect and affection long after I moved out of their home in Ferme. I celebrated two happy events with them. Lumi had looked forward to her wedding day for a long time. Her fiancé, Fatos, was a professional soldier from Tirana. For most of their special day, Lumi sat perched in silence on a hard-backed chair in Lavdosh and Kosta's lounge. Dressed in a white wedding dress, she received female visitors who sat with her for a time, but few words were exchanged. It was considered to be a solemn moment, because the bride's life under her parents' roof was about to come to an end. More than that, she and her husband were ultimately to live in America, thanks to winning the necessary papers in a lottery! In due course, Lavdosh and the remaining members of his family were also to leave Albania – in their case, to reside in Athens. In the evening of their wedding day, Lumi and Fatos, both looking very sombre at first, made their way to a hired hall a few yards from her family home. Normally, it contained an old, well-used billiard table. On this night, dining tables had been erected to accommodate the eighty or so guests. Throughout the evening, everyone feasted on spit-roasted goat meat. Every few minutes, people would approach the top table, on which I'd been invited to sit, to pass on their best wishes to the bride and groom. They carried their drinks with them and clinked glasses with all members of the wedding party. I, too, was toasted, as many people saw me as an honorary member of the bride's family. Kosta sang a beautiful song, which likened her daughter to moonlight shining on freshly fallen snow. Guests, accompanied by a deep humming, rendered many other songs. As the evening drew to a close, one of the guests leaned out of a window and fired a gun up into the night sky. The celebratory gesture was the signal for Fatos and Lumi to leave.

A few moments after I arrived back home, there was a knock at my door. It was Fatos, along with his best man and two other male members of his party. Apparently, he wasn't permitted to sleep with his bride until a re-run of the day's activities was played out with his side of the family, the following day in Tirana.

'Can I have a bed for the night?' he said.

That was the first time in my life I had shared a room with a groom on his wedding night! The following morning, he gratefully accepted a disposable razor from me and, after preparing himself to face the world, went on his way.

The other cause for celebration had been a birth in the family. I was given the honour of 'christening' the new arrival, a baby calf. I had recently been sent a tape of Bruce Springsteen music, so 'Bruce' it was.

* * *

Friends from England, all paying their own way, were
keen to support me in gently reaching out to the people
of Borsh. To overcome the language barrier, I followed
up a recommendation, made by my Dutch friends, to
contact a church in a different part of the country. It was
blessed with a large contingent of English-speaking students; many of them were willing to spend a few days in
Borsh as translators. A programme of neighbourhood
visits began. We had to proceed with care, the veil of
mystique that surrounded my friends, and more particularly myself, could not be snatched away in a moment.
Few, if any, of the people we visited would have understood my reasons for going to live in their village.
Aesthetic beauty was one thing, struggling to live with a
crumbling infrastructure made life far from romantic.
Many questioned why anyone in his right mind would
choose to live in a country that was at least fifty years
behind the times. They were entitled to an explanation;
more than that, unless there was some acceptance of the
messenger, his message would never be seriously considered. 'Bible thumping' would not have been helpful.
Tradition had it that Borsh wore a Muslim badge, even
though there was little evidence of any form of religious
practice.

In most cases, interest was expressed in the Christian
faith, but accepting that it was relevant to their own situations was at least several more steps away. Many
prayers were offered concerning current family anxieties, as well as for the healing of past hurts. We carried
Albanian print copies of St John's gospel to distribute as
we saw fit.

For most of those who came to visit, there was a special moment. These often arrived quite out of the blue.

For Peter, a retired factory worker, an abiding memory was provided by a woman we came across as we walked along a hillside track. Sara, who was digging beside a gravel bank, greeted us with a warm smile. Without hesitation, she invited all eight of us into her humble home for refreshments. Coffee, *raki*, which was a home-made brew of distilled grapes, Turkish delight and a type of jam were served on round silver-coloured trays. As was the custom, she sussed out that Peter was the senior member of the group and served him first, then the others, in descending age order. How many of us would instantly invite a group of strangers into our home and then proceed to give them the best things out of the kitchen cupboard? Peter was left watery eyed after Sara told us that it was the first time she had ever entertained foreigners; it was a day she would never forget.

Not all team visits went well. Far from every group complementing and building upon the work of another, the experiences encountered during the visit of an English youth group, revealed just how well-founded my initial misgivings had been. Despite the warnings of 'danger ahead', twenty-six people, including translators, crammed into my home, designed to sleep a maximum of twelve. Tomfoolery amongst the male members of the team caused lots of headaches. They were to bridge-building with my neighbours what the Vikings had been to the early church in Britain. A series of time-consuming hospital trips to Saranda became necessary. A scorpion stung one teenage boy as he slept on the kitchen floor; it was painful for him, but not fatal. Another was hospitalized after an epileptic attack was induced by the ill-disciplined behaviour of some of his friends. I had to take yet another boy to hospital after he fell and hit his head on the floor; he suffered concussion. Unfortunately, worse was to come.

Two female members of the group were attacked one day, as they made their way from the shoreline, through the orchard, towards home. The senior leader of the team and I had a meeting in Saranda, regarding an appointment at the end of their trip. The group had subsequently been left in the charge of several junior leaders. Despite my express instructions to the contrary, two of the girls were given permission to leave the main party. Some men in a lorry made a nuisance of themselves as the girls began walking. To their initial relief, the people in the lorry beat a hasty retreat when a man, who went on to describe himself as a policeman, came to their rescue. In pidgin English, he asked them where they were going and volunteered to show them a short cut. Arriving at a remote spot, he turned nasty and tried to sexually assault them. They successfully resisted his advances, and finally got free of him when they had the presence of mind to offer him the jewellery they were wearing, which he accepted. As if to add legitimacy to the abhorrent incident, he shook hands with them both before disappearing.

Although the perpetrator of the crime was identified shortly afterwards, justice proved to be elusive. He was beaten up by one of his brothers in the presence of a policeman and me. This was seen to be the end of the matter by the local law enforcers – a course of action I did not condone. On pursuing matters further, I received subtle threats regarding my personal safety. The advice received, from reliable official sources in Tirana, was that my efforts to secure justice would ultimately prove to be fruitless. Furthermore, I would be obliged to leave the country permanently, to escape the consequences of upsetting the wrong people. For their part, the two girls involved showed commendable maturity and strength of character. Immediately afterwards, I transferred all female members of the party to a safe location, away from Borsh, for the duration of their stay.

The sweltering heat of my first summer in Borsh, somewhat compensated for by beautiful starlit nights, gave way to wave after wave of autumnal thunderstorms. As they rolled around the mountains, torrential rain poured, sometimes for many days at a time. Although the downpours brought even more power cuts, there was also the promise of brighter intervals. I met Bujar Allushi, another English speaker, from the seaside neighbourhood of Shkalle. An economics graduate, his company was light and refreshing. One of five brothers and two sisters, he was helping the family build a guesthouse just a few yards from the sea's edge. Bujar agreed to be my translator for the proposed gatherings I had planned, in the heart of a small community of northerners. They had taken up residency in and around a former prison building at the most southerly tip of the village. I regularly called in at the family home of Nikol and Maria. With their origins in the northern town of Pukë, they carried a Catholic tradition in their blood. It was in their home that the forthcoming informal meetings were to be hosted.

Food often figured at some point during my visits. One day, as I was leaving, their oldest son escorted me to the rickety wooden gate.

'Do you like our pig?' he asked. A huge sow was lying on the path, basking in the afternoon sunshine. When I said, 'Yes,' he responded by saying, 'Good, one day we'll eat it together.'

I missed English food, especially on the days when I was faced with a dish of cold cow's giblets soup. Imagine my excitement when I was invited by Nikol to join his family for a turkey lunch! In the event, I enjoyed our time together, but things didn't work out quite as I'd anticipated. I hope I managed to conceal my horror when, instead of white, succulent slices of turkey meat, I was served the turkey's lungs! As I made the long walk home, I couldn't help but smile ruefully to myself about what might have been.

Unfortunately, before the weekly get-togethers got under way, or I could enjoy a decent bacon sandwich, everything changed. Trouble had been simmering between the northerners and the rest of the village over land rights. Were the outsiders legally entitled to be occupying the land they were on? A line of demarcation was drawn and Bujar refused to cross that line. The start date for our gatherings had to be put on an indefinite hold.

The acquisition of a mobile phone brought with it the promise of a huge leap forward in communications. Before public telephones were available, I would sometimes ask the occasional British-looking tourist, in Saranda on a day trip, if he or she would mind contacting my family on their return to England. This was to pass on the message that all was well. If willing, I would give the messenger a couple of pounds to cover the cost. Obtaining a mobile phone from Corfu, in the days before 'pay and go', wasn't straightforward. As with opening a bank account for money transfers from England, there were many hoops to jump through. I soon became acquainted with the word, 'avrio', meaning tomorrow.

Unfortunately, the new phone didn't work terribly well. I tried various locations across Borsh, some of them several miles apart, in my attempts to find a good spot for capturing a signal. Calls to the church office, where Clare Stradling was one of the early missions co-ordinators, or to my family, didn't last more than two or three seconds. A place where I found relative success was halfway up a steep-sided hill. In the ever-curious eyes of the villagers, the sight of me furtively clutching a phone in one hand with bits of paper and a pen in the other, added to their suspicions. A man called Beço, who grew vegetables on a nearby plot of land, watched me with particular interest. He put it about the village that I was making surreptitious phone calls to a secret lover, because I'd go to a secluded location to make the contacts.

Occasionally, stepping out of the locals' gaze provided a welcome change of scene. However, my interest in seeing Tirana wasn't satisfied at the first attempt. The vehicle I was travelling in crashed into the back of a horse and cart, on a well-used road near to a town called Fier. Such road users were commonplace, vying for space with cars, lorries, mopeds, sheep, goats and the occasional pig. A crowd quickly gathered, but couldn't decide whether the presence of a foreigner represented a moneymaking opportunity or not. A fight broke out and a man brandishing a knife fell onto his own blade. Whilst the scuffle was in full swing, I was able to slip away. I later heard that the man with the knife wound was not seriously hurt and the horse only suffered bruising to its bottom.

My next attempt to see Tirana was eventful for different reasons. A missionary umbrella organisation, 'Albanian Encouragement Project', operated a small private aircraft service between the capital and Saranda. A journey that took numerous hours by road lasted only forty minutes in their five-seater plane, so for $40 I tried it out. My Dutch pal, Jasper, and I stood and waited in a flat field just out of town. The small plane's first approach had to be aborted because of sheep grazing on the landing strip.

Soon we were on our way, enjoying fine views of the mountain hamlets far below. As we came in to land at

Tirana Airport, a man casually cycled across the runway just a hundred yards ahead of us; he was carrying a car windscreen under one of his arms.

'Welcome to Tirana,' said Dave, our American pilot.

The return journey by road seemed endless. For hour upon hour we weaved around one pothole after another. In every town was the miserable spectacle of people sat behind a few tins of motor oil or a tray of cigarettes for sale. As they sat there, hands thrust into pockets, some wearing woollen balaclavas, my heart went out to them. I wondered how many hours they had to sit there, in the bone-numbing cold, to make just a few pennies.

Not long before I flew back to England for a break, Eqerem told me something that appeared to have little consequence at the time. He referred to a savings scheme his brother had mentioned to me several months earlier. Lavdosh had inquired about rates of interest given on investments in England. He had laughed when I told him that they ran at between 2 and 3 per cent, saying that he'd found a way of doubling his money within months. Eqerem told me that his brother had now lost all of his savings in the scheme. I didn't know it then, but a touch paper had been lit.

* * *

A few days later I was on a plane back to England. I would cherish visits home and tried to squeeze every last drop out of the precious time available.

With the arrival of twins, Hannah and Rebekah, my brother Vin and his wife became parents for the first time. During a false alarm, a couple of days before their birth, Vin had driven Bev to hospital. Not one to easily be put on the back foot, he insisted that they stopped en route to enjoy fish and chips at his in-laws'.

One late January morning, *The Times* newspaper carried a photograph and an article about civil protests in Durres, Albania. I read it with particular interest. Albania's parliament had passed a law, banning pyramid investment schemes, a get rich quick scam, which also introduced a twenty-year jail sentence for operators. I thought about Lavdosh and his lost savings. Three days later, the same newspaper spoke of Albania's government, under the leadership of President Sali Berisha, being under considerable threat. Violent riots threatened to engulf Albania. Soldiers with machine-guns were reported to have been deployed in the capital, some of which were called to guard government buildings. Tens of thousands of protesters clashed with riot police in Skanderberg Square and the Boulevard of the Martyrs. Protestors demonstrating at the football stadium in a town called Lushnje, in the middle of the country, set about Albania's Foreign Minister. Once seized, Triton Shehu was dragged along by his tie and had an onion stuffed in his mouth as a mark of humiliation. President Berisha appealed for calm. The catalyst for the trouble was the savings schemes. Like Lavdosh, thousands of Albanian's had fallen prey to the tricksters who'd found easy pickings in a land where the average wage at that time was £35 a month. Some commentators stated that seven out of ten families had lost their savings. Many were said to have sold their livestock, land and homes to obtain the money to invest. What snapped the people's patience was the fraudsters' visibly cosy relationship with government ministers and high profile contributors to party coffers. Questions were also being raised over the legitimacy of the government's last election victory.

From the relative comfort of England, Albania's troubles seemed far away. Before returning, there were gifts to shop for, such as the pair of black shoes Kosta had asked me to get for her.

When the time came for me to return to Albania, I felt extremely sorry to be leaving. England represented order, the good things in life; it was where my family and true friends resided. However, nothing could have stopped me from returning. Recent newspaper stories had been worrying, but they focused on events many hours away from the relative tranquillity of Borsh. The latest press reports spoke of protest leaders, labelled 'Red Terrorists' by government leaders, being rounded up. This gave me high hopes for a calming of tensions within the country. Telephone conversations to friends in or around Albania gave no cause for me to reconsider my return. I felt that it was necessary to demonstrate my commitment to the villagers by being alongside them through difficult times.

* * *

A friendly resident of Ferme invited me to his family home for a supper of salami and eggs not long after I'd arrived back from England. I was persuaded to spend the night there, but didn't get much sleep. I shared a room with my host's father, an 82-year-old partisan from World War II. I was kept awake by the sound of his missile-like projectiles hitting the spittoon, inconveniently located near to where my head was resting.

During the following days, a steady trickle of children came knocking on my door. They requested copies of the colourful books of Bible stories I kept on a long shelf just inside the house. One little girl, the 9-year-old granddaughter of a neighbour, noticed some dirty dishes in a bowl at the end of my hallway. She instinctively asked if she could do the washing up for me.

If the ebb and flow of village life remained relatively unchanged, the same could not be said for all parts of the country. BBC World Service radio news reports began to regularly feature stories from Albania. I became increasingly captivated by the bulletins, so whenever possible made sure I was near to my radio just before the hour mark. The broadcasts provided me with a reliable source of information. Little by little, law and order melted away. Vlore was described as a rebel town, which no longer recognized its MPs or mayor. A police station had been burned down, following the bloody break-up of a hunger strike.

One night, the troubles afflicting many other areas spilled over into Borsh. As darkness fell, towards the end of an otherwise unremarkable day, I was at home drinking an uninspiring mug of soup. For the first time in my life I heard live machine-gun fire. I didn't immediately rush to a window, but when several other guns were discharged I went out onto the balcony. I could barely believe my eyes. Someone was firing tracer bullets skywards and distress flares were being launched from a place nearby. On going back inside, I locked the balcony door and turned all the lights off. Since first going to live there, life appeared to have been turned on its head, but this was even more incredible. I went to lie on my bed, listening to the intensifying sound of gunfire outside. Just as I was beginning to think that, as the only foreigner around, I may be in some danger, I saw Eqerem's flashlight shining as he came down my path.

'Don't worry,' he said. 'You have nothing to be frightened of, no one here wishes you harm. The people have taken all the guns from an army base not far from here and now they are just trying them out.'

He stayed and chatted for a while, but then, as he was leaving, said something that undid all of his good work in trying to reassure me.

'Don't forget, you have absolutely nothing to worry about,' he repeated, then added, 'but be sure to sleep on the bottom bunk and stay away from the windows!'

It felt strange to be doing something as normal as getting ready for bed, when outside it sounded as if World War III had broken out. But what other course of action would have been more appropriate? I offered a word of prayer and went on to sleep soundly.

The following morning all was quiet. Not knowing what to expect, I made my way to the top of the path. I decided to take a short walk along the road; from there I was able to look down into the village centre. As I passed one of the houses, a boy living there greeted me in his usual cheery manner. However, he was wearing a gas mask! A friend by his side was playing with a military radio set. Their mood was one of excitement, as was the case with several young men I saw during my short foray outside. I returned home and stayed there for the rest of the day, listening to radio news reports. Army depots all over the country had been looted. The picture being painted was one I likened to a series of supermarket trolley dashes. In this case, however, substitute frozen turkeys and tinned salmon for bullets and hand grenades!

Given the circumstances, one might think that staying indoors was the only option, but that wasn't the case. I was able to move about the village, even though things were now very different. It appeared that just about everybody had helped themselves to whatever military hardware they could lay their hands on.

As soon as I felt confident enough to visit Shkalle, in order to make calls home, I set off walking there one morning. A lorry pulled up alongside me, driven by Sali, a powerfully built man, with regulation stubble on his chin. I accepted the offer of a lift and was pulled up into the cab by his friend, Afrim. The two men delighted in showing me some huge shell cases in a box resting on the dashboard.

Sali said, 'If you want any guns or bullets, we can fix you up.'

I wondered if acceptance of their generous offer would have been conducive to my work of communicating the message of God's love for all people. I told them that I'd leave it for the time being, but thanked them just the same.

Fortunately, the wind was blowing in the right direction, so I was able to get a decent telephone signal.

Someone at church told me that British Embassy advice was to try and get north. In fact, the suggestion wasn't practical. Supplies of diesel had dried up and it was evident that few people were using the roads. I had seen very little traffic pass through the village since the first night of gunfire. On the contrary, the advice from the locals was always the same, 'Stay put.' Many of them insisted that I was safe within the confines of the village, whereas travelling on the roads was very dangerous. The general consensus was, 'If you stay here with us, we will protect you.'

I thought a telephone call to my family would settle any concerns they may have had for my safety. Unfortunately, this didn't go entirely as I'd hoped. To diffuse my mother's anxieties, I decided to keep the conversation to normal, everyday things. I started to ask her about a recipe for bread and butter pudding. At home I had a small mountain of lemons and oranges given to me by friends in the village. During the relaying of baking instructions, someone discharged a machine-gun into the sea just a few yards from where I was standing. After a moment of silence, Mom asked if that was machine-gun fire she had just heard. I told her it was nothing to worry about. An awkward pause followed, then she said, 'Are you taking your vitamin tablets?'

On a different day, I was walking to Shkalle when I came across a teenager sitting behind an anti-aircraft gun.

'I think I can reach Corfu from here,' he said. 'What do you think, Riçardi?'

Jokingly I said, 'Only use cowpats if you do.'

As I walked on, I imagined how my report back to church would have read for that day, 'Today I helped a local boy shell sun-bathing tourists in Corfu with cowpats...'

Further down the road, some men in a car stopped me. They had the idea of trying to frighten me, so the front passenger aimed a gun in my direction and asked for $10. I made a non-committal reply and they all roared with laughter. Before driving off, the man with the gun pointed out that I was standing in a muddy puddle.

Of greater seriousness was an accident that occurred in a different neighbourhood, as I was passing through several days later. I heard a scream and ran up to the door of the house where the noise came from. Klodjana, who was 15 years old, had been hit a glancing blow to her collarbone, by a stray bullet her brother had been playing with. Although she wasn't seriously wounded, her mother was understandably distressed. After I had been in their home for a couple of minutes, Klodjana's mother disappeared into a back room. She returned with a small glass dish of boiled sweets to offer me. Such a gesture of hospitality in this moment of crisis spoke volumes. At that time, the world was watching television pictures of Albanians firing machine-guns into the air, many wearing macho bandanas. However, it was the incident inside Klodjana's home that reflected the truer character of the people I was beginning to get to know.

3

UP, UP AND AWAY

'This tank is all I've got.'

A man who'd spent five years working in Greece had lost everything he'd owned in the ill-fated savings schemes. He was sitting in a looted tank in Gjirokaster, the nearest town to Saranda, telling an Albanian television news reporter that he was prepared to fight those responsible for his losses. In the eyes of those watching with me in my neighbour's living room, he created an amusing spectacle and his words provoked laughter.

'Oh Shqiptar!' said Eqerem, meaning 'O Albanian!' as if to feign a rebuke, whilst secretly admiring him.

Television news pictures of an ancient battleship being sailed around Saranda Bay typified numerous images of non-military personnel trying out the country's entire arsenal of weapons.

Some local young men had the idea of setting up a type of vigilante post near to the bridge that spans a sometimes dried up river bed below. It was at a village border point, so the would-be vigilantes were able to observe anyone approaching. My Land Rover was considered to be just right for their purposes, so they stole it from outside the house. In Lavdosh's van, along with several gun-brandishing well-wishers, we searched the neighbouring villages, but returned to Eqerem's home empty handed.

Zuli greeted us and said, 'I've found it! It's down by the bridge.'

During an angry confrontation, Eqerem slapped several faces and strong words were exchanged, but in the end the vehicle was recovered.

There was a bizarre element to the episode. In the back of the vehicle I had one or two fake fingers and some plastic noses, purchased from a joke shop in England several months earlier. I thought they might come in useful when spending time with the village children. I wondered what my vigilante friends thought when they came across them? They were missing when I searched the vehicle in the morning light next day. Some of the windows had been smashed out, presumably a modification made to create gun turrets.

I was free to walk about the village as I pleased but, inevitably, the chances of getting involved in an accident, however unintentional, gradually increased. One day I was walking through the Haliq neighbourhood when someone started firing a rifle. I could hear the bullets whistling past my ears and sheltered in some trees, below the path. A shepherd, giving his sheep some welcome shade from the sun, muttered under his breath about 'a silly donkey firing a gun'. After a few minutes, he told me that it would be safe to continue on my way.

Despite assurances that I would be quite safe if I 'stayed put', it didn't simply rest there. There were many factors to consider. I did feel safe amongst the villagers, but what about if a stranger came to take me hostage? The established forces of law and order had broken down and that threat wasn't something I could rule out. The very offer of protection from my neighbours complicated things. What if an outsider came to take me and a friend got in the way of a bullet whilst coming to my assistance? If there was, in fact, a safe corridor of exit that existed, wouldn't I be crazy to ignore it? Furthermore, I didn't want to try to appear brave by remaining in a dangerous place when I should have quietly slipped away for a time.

On the other hand, what of the Christian faith I was endeavouring to share? Is it something that's only relevant during times when life is smooth and crinkle-free? What message would my abandonment when the chips were down give to others? I talked to Bujar about this and he said he would try and get into Saranda, to establish if that safe passage existed or not.

I felt a chill go down my spine when Bujar told me, one day, that three members of the 'Shikh', the secret police, were in the village, to gather intelligence on behalf of the government about local troublemakers. Bujar warned me never to enter my house alone once it was dark and not to answer the door at night. For me, personally, that unseen threat was the most sinister development during the crisis.

I was making regular telephone calls back to England, but Bujar rightly suggested that I made them from inside his home. There I would be away from the gaze of others, who may have got jumpy about a foreigner making overseas calls.

Back in England, the media, both local and national, had approached my brother for updates on my situation. Vin told BBC Radio's *Five Live* that their request for a telephone link-up with me wasn't something he was willing to sanction. He didn't want me to be exposed to unnecessary attention – in particular, to sinister forces in Albania, who may have been listening in.

Against a backdrop of nationwide mounting disorder, everyday matters such as Bujar and younger brother Ilir's first catch of fish from their new rubber inflatable boat, provided welcome distractions.

'We want you to share our first fish with us,' said Bujar.

His sister, Angela, started frying, and I went upstairs, into an empty room to plug in my phone. Keeping any sort of decent charge in it was a constant challenge. Just as I plugged it in Vin called. He was unusually brief. Would I phone Gary at church because he needed to speak to me urgently? Gary sounded bright and excited. What he went on to tell me was remarkable.

'The SAS are waiting to come and get you! *HMS Birmingham* is moored somewhere off the Albanian coast and you are to phone them.'

After checking whether he was joking or not, I made the call. The major I spoke to was friendly in his manner.

'We'd like to send a helicopter in to pick you up,' he told me.

I told him about the anti-aircraft gun situated along the shoreline and expressed misgivings about his proposal. The major said that the chances of it being used skilfully were slim, since locals were manning it.

'Army conscription is compulsory here,' I told him. 'So it's quite likely that certain people will have experience of operating one,' I continued. I went on to reassure him that I wasn't in any immediate danger. He appreciated the information and advised me to remain in regular contact with the British Embassy in Tirana. Before finishing the call he took a note of my mobile phone number.

I went downstairs and began to enjoy my fried fish.

'Gezuar!' we toasted, meaning, 'Cheers!' and I took a sip of cool beer from my glass.

Isn't it amazing how the phone always goes during mealtimes? Well, it happened then . . . the fact that it was the SAS calling back made it excusable. The same man said that a revised plan, one in which they would drive down from Tirana, avoiding Vlore, drive me back up and then fly me out to Italy, was being considered. I agreed that I would be in a location where I could be sure of getting a telephone signal the following morning at 10 a.m., so that we could confirm arrangements.

As I made my way home later that afternoon, I stopped to watch some boys kicking around a semi-deflated plastic football on some rough open ground. A policeman called Altin came over and talked with me. Since the army depots had been looted a fortnight earlier, the police had gone to ground, but as of the following day, they were to report back for duty all over the country.

When I got home it occurred to me that I could be about to spend my last night there for a while and I felt a deep sadness. I thought of the three young children that regularly came to visit me and decided to take some chocolate down to their house. Their mother was chasing three errant sheep around the garden when I arrived.

'I've come to say goodbye,' I told them.

The children said that they understood why I had to go and reached up to kiss me. As I was leaving, their mother said that they would all join her husband, who was working in Greece, as soon as possible.

Once back home, I turned the radio on. My favourite football team, Wolverhampton Wanderers, had lost 3–2 away at Oldham. I ate a tea of tinned tuna, spring onions, red peppers and bread. My breath would later smell horribly but there was nobody there to complain. As I lay in bed my world seemed surreal. Reports of armed looters roaming the country, boys playing football, little children's faces, the SAS coming for me, calls home to Gary, Vin and Mom . . . I wondered what the coming days would hold.

I didn't sleep well that night; my mind was turning over many things. By the time I got up at 6 a.m., I'd already made a mental list of household items I thought would be more secure if stored next door at Eqerem's house during my forthcoming absence. My kettle, toaster and decent kitchen utensils were packed away into boxes.

Later, as I walked towards Shkalle, where I knew I'd get a good telephone signal, an elderly woman approached me.

'You're still here! You are very strong for staying,' she told me. Ironically, in a few moments I would be discussing the details of my departure with the British military.

At exactly 10 a.m. my phone rang. I was standing next to a concrete bunker. Nearby, a large cow on the stony beach gazed dolefully at me. The female voice on the other end of the phone said that she was calling from Hereford, England. I was to call the British Embassy in Tirana.

When I finally got through, the gentleman I spoke to asked me to describe the immediate geography of the Borsh area. This was to ascertain where would be a good meeting point at 8 a.m. the next day. I described the bridge over the dried up riverbed. I was told that men driving two green or white open-topped Land Rovers, small Union Jack stickers displayed on the windscreens, would meet me there. The men would be armed but wearing non-military garb. I had no need to worry; they would take good care of me. I was asked to describe myself and what I would be wearing. The major, his manner precise but not austere, asked me if I knew a British Eco Tourism worker living in the next village? He may like a lift out too. I undertook to make contact with him.

'Please don't give details of who we are or what we've discussed to anyone,' he told me.

I couldn't get hold of Gary by telephone because the church office was by now besieged with press enquiries. During a conversation with Vin, my spirit was lifted because, far from my pending departure representing failure, he could foresee how the interest in my situation could be used positively for the wider purposes of our mission. I also telephoned Mom and Doug. Feeling sure of their integrity, I knew I could tell them what was to happen the next day.

Mom, a great health food enthusiast, advised, 'Don't forget to take a ginger capsule; it will help settle your stomach for the journey.'

As promised, I went in search of the man the Special Forces major had spoken of. It was a long, hot walk up the hill to Qeparo. After making enquiries, I found Robert Reynolds, a teacher, in his late thirties. He was impressed at the concern our embassy was showing for our welfare and said he would come too. His colleague, Evelyn, said that she would join us, but in the event changed her mind. She lived to tell the tale.

That night Bujar came to wish me all the best.

'What shall I tell the people back home about the Albanians?' I asked him.

After a moment or two he gave his reply, 'Tell them that all the Albanian people want is a true democracy. When a child tells its father, "I am hungry," what is the father to do?'

My second visitor that night was Eqerem. He brought me a Kalashnikov, a Russian made automatic rifle. It was to use in case I encountered problems with people trying to steal the Land Rover again. In reality, I'd have thought twice about even using an egg whisk in anger, let alone a Kalashnikov rifle. As he was leaving, BBC World Service news reported that President Berisha had granted a pardon to Fatos Nano, a Socialist Party champion being held in a political prison.

The morning of 17 March 1997 started ordinarily enough for me. I went for my usual jog, choosing the uphill route towards the tiny neighbourhood of Kriz. After showering, I called in at Eqerem's to hand him his Kalashnikov back. It had spent the night resting on my kitchen work surface. Zuli made me a cup of Turkish coffee and gave me a dish of *kos*, a type of yoghurt, to eat. We exchanged farewells, and then I walked down to the bridge as per yesterday's telephone conversation with the army major. Along the way, I called in at a house to drop off a couple of books I'd promised to the small boys who lived there.

When I got to the bridge, Robert Reynolds was just arriving. His translator, who was pushing a bicycle, accompanied him. At 8 a.m. sharp, two open-topped Land Rovers drove down the hill towards us.

'Richard Welch?' the passenger in the first vehicle asked.

After brief handshakes we clambered in and were on our way. Our front passenger, a man in his mid- to late twenties and powerfully built, held a camera in his hands. As we drove by one bunker after another, situated along the scenic coastline, he expressed great interest in what he saw. He then proceeded to take several photographs. I, too, had my camera in my pocket, so I asked him if there would be any objection to me taking photographs of whatever was going to happen that morning.

'Not at all, as long as you don't sell them to *The Sun* newspaper,' he quipped.

The morning was brilliantly clear and still. We drove through Qeparo, then on towards a place called Palermos, the location I'd described as being a potentially good landing spot during my interrupted fish lunch a couple of days earlier.

I'd noticed a helicopter hovering high above; apparently, the men in the front of our vehicle were in radio contact with it. Some fifteen minutes into the journey, just as we approached the Palermos Bay area, our vehicles came to a standstill. Several people brandishing guns were manning a roadblock. One of the men in the first Land Rover spoke fluent Albanian and in a few moments it was smiles all round.

'We like the English,' said one of the gunmen and enthusiastically waved us through.

Seconds later, to my amazement, two Chinook helicopters suddenly dropped down from the sky, creating a cloud of dust as they descended. They touched down on a narrow strip of land that joins the road to an island castle. As they landed, twenty armed soldiers ran out from the open bellies of the helicopters. They knelt on the ground holding their guns as we drove between them. I noticed that the soldiers had mouthpieces attached and presumably they had earpieces under their helmets. It was a moment I didn't want to miss and I reached for my camera.

'*This wouldn't be a good time to leave the lens cover on,*' I thought to myself.

Almost immediately, the soldiers were given the order to get back inside. The helicopters were only on the ground for a maximum of thirty seconds. As we took off, I looked back to get a brief glimpse of the people manning the roadblock. They were looking up with mouths wide open in astonishment.

The combined roar of the engine and rotary blades made conversation difficult. We remained sitting in the Land Rover throughout. Slowly, my eyes became accustomed to the poor light. I watched the soldiers' faces as we surged up and down. One of them pointed towards some sick bags hanging on the fuselage and Robert reached for one. The journey made him very sick. More time passed and the same soldier stepped forward again, this time holding earplugs. I pretended to think that they were sweets to eat and he laughed. Our front passenger turned to check on our welfare every so often and apologized about the bumpy ride. He was good-natured towards us and we shared a joke about being disappointed that there wasn't an 'in-flight movie' to watch. We landed very briefly in Tirana, I think, before taking off again. My guess was that British Embassy personnel had disembarked from the other helicopter. The man in the front seat turned to speak to me again.

'We will land shortly on an American aircraft carrier for refuelling. We haven't got permission to do that with non military personnel on board,' he shouted into my left ear. 'If they ask you any questions, tell them you're one of us doing undercover duties.'

I just nodded and tried to give the impression that it was the sort of thing I regularly took in my stride. Through a small aperture in the fuselage I had occasional glimpses of the ship below, against the deep blue Adriatic Sea. As we landed I was told, 'OK, we've got to get out now, remember what I said to you.' I relayed the message to Robert, but in fact the American Forces didn't question us. We were all ushered into a type of hangar and the men in charge gave a signal for all the British soldiers to put their guns down on the deck. We were all counted several times and after some twenty minutes were told we could re-board the helicopters.

From there we flew into an Italian Air Force base at Gjoia del Colle, north of Taranto. Still sitting in the Land Rover, we were driven off the helicopter and into a huge hangar. Inside were dozens of neatly laid out foam mattresses, with kit bags alongside. Our driver told us to help ourselves to cups of tea from a nearby urn, while those engaged in the operation went to be debriefed in a far corner of the hangar.

'How many of these soldiers belong to Special Forces?' I asked our driver.

'All of us,' was the reply.

We were shown around the base and invited to have lunch. It had been a tremendously exciting few hours and I hadn't thought of food since eating Zuli's *kos* earlier that morning. In the canteen, some of the soldiers involved in our operation came and sat next to me as I tucked into a jacket potato, fish and green beans. Their mood was light and self-effacing, which made this highly competent group of people all the more impressive, in my opinion. I thanked them for what they had done but they made light of it all. They joked about football allegiances. One was a Leicester City supporter and was looking forward to what used to be called 'The League Cup Final' the following weekend.

'Let's hope someone tells him the score,' another joked, 'because he can't read or write!' Then it was my turn to be on the receiving end of some leg-pulling.

'So what do you do in Albania then?'

I went on to explain a little of my work.

The soldier who'd passed me the earplugs in the helicopter said, 'Well, you've blown it now, haven't you? You've deserted them!' He said nothing that I hadn't already turned over in my mind several times. I was sure, despite being reluctant to accept it, that my course of action to pull out of Albania for the time being was the correct one.

A dark-haired man, with slightly pointed features, wearing combat fatigues, approached me as I walked away from the canteen after lunch. He held a hand out to me and said, 'I'd been hoping for an opportunity to speak with you. I was your pilot this morning.'

I thanked him for his trouble as I shook his hand.

'Not at all,' he said. 'Most of our daily routine involves practising and it becomes monotonous week after week. Today was the most fun we've had for ages!'

I asked him why we'd flown so low all the way up to Tirana.

'We actually flew at around fifty feet above ground level because the less visible we are from a distance the better. Anyone on the ground who had the idea of firing a gun at us would have had more chance of hitting their target if we were high in the sky. As it was, we came and went before the people on the ground could blink.'

I asked him if anyone had, in fact, fired at us. He said that the helicopter monitoring the Borsh to Palermos leg of the exercise reported a single shot being fired, but it didn't do any harm.

'I think they're trying to sort out a flight back to England in a Hercules for you. If not, you'll be able to spend the night here,' he said. He, too, took an interest in what I was doing in Albania and he wished me all the best for the future, before going for his lunch.

Later that afternoon, the Italian Consulate liaised with the British Consulate. After being driven the forty kilometres to Bari Airport by a member of the support staff in an unmarked saloon car, we were met by a Consulate official. Tickets for a domestic flight to Rome, with a subsequent flight to Heathrow were purchased.

Robert Reynolds and I landed in London at 8.10 p.m. He said that he'd call friends to come and pick him up. We wished each other well before parting and he said it was unlikely he would ever return to Albania. I hired a car and drove up to Vin and Bev's home in Dudley. Upon arriving, I had to knock on their front door several times because they had all gone to bed for the night. After eventually making Vin hear, he welcomed me home and wearily laid a mattress down on the lounge floor for me to sleep on. One of the most incredible days of my life came to an end.

* * *

A next-door neighbour of Vin's was a newspaper reporter. My dramatic departure from Albania was something he wanted to talk about the next day.

The story spread. Local television news recorded an interview with me during a hastily convened press conference, which Gary also attended. The national press, including *The Times*, carried the story, with a photograph of me, on its front page. My fleeting moment of notoriety was a little incomplete however; not all of the papers got my name right. I was interviewed on nat-ional television twice. The first of those two extremely nerve-wracking experiences was for a satirical comedy magazine programme for Channel 4. Evidently it also carried a topical news story. As I walked down the corridor from 'The Green Room' to the studio, I passed a long queue of people who were to make up the live studio audience. My heart was pounding.

'Don't worry, Richard,' said news producer Danielle Graham, 'it's only television!'

I felt that the interview I gave was flat and uninspiring. The heat of the studio lights was intense and I was wet with perspiration when I left the stage. On after me was Jeremy Beadle, a late replacement for Jerry Hall who'd cancelled at the last minute.

After the programme, I chatted to someone who looked vaguely familiar. I wondered where I'd seen him before. He turned out to be Mark Little of *Neighbours* and

Big Breakfast fame. A favourite moment came when a man in his twenties, wearing a denim jacket, approached me and shook my hand. He went on to explain that his girlfriend worked as a make-up artist for the television studio and he regularly received complimentary tickets for the show.

'What you said really touched my heart,' he said.

Perhaps something positive came out of the interview after all.

Steve Chalke interviewed me for his Sunday programme on GMTV a few days later. I felt that this interview was more successful than the previous one.

Then Barbara Myers interviewed me at Bush House, London, for her current affairs programme, *Outlook*, on BBC World Service radio. On arrival, I was given a sticky-backed visitor's badge, which was dated, and had the number 1683 stamped on it.

'We'll have about as much time to do this interview as it takes to boil an egg,' she told me. A microphone hung down from the ceiling and was situated midway between us.

'You're a natural broadcaster,' she beamed at the end. 'We don't need to do any editing; we'll broadcast it as it is.'

As I was preparing to leave she said, 'You might be interested in meeting our colleagues from the BBC's Albanian section.'

Ten minutes later I was drinking coffee with three members of their news team. They were keen to interview me and would broadcast it on the Albanian airwaves the following day. It was an interview that went particularly well. I explained my reasons for living in Albania and talked about my favourable experiences of village life, including Klodjana's mother with her dish of boiled sweets. My desire was to return to Borsh as soon as possible.

I had no way of knowing at the time just how crucial that relatively low-key interview was. It had come during a round of higher profile engagements, but in terms of serving the purpose of our mission, it was arguably more significant than all of the others put together. The manner of my departure had apparently spread like wildfire across south-west Albania. Many people had concluded that I was a spy.

'His government would not send helicopters to collect him if he was just a normal citizen,' they said. I would not have been welcomed back.

However, when the interview was transmitted into Albania, those hearing it changed their minds. Several years after the broadcast, people still delighted in telling me, 'We heard you say some very good things about us on the radio. We now know you have come as a friend.'

4

DONKEY ON THE THIRD FLOOR

Not returning to Albania was never an option. I'd given considerable thought and prayer to moving there in the first place and the recent troubles would be no more than an interruption. An immediate return would have been foolhardy, so for several weeks I stayed in England where, amongst other things, I spent time in and around our partner churches. Times spent with Gary, back at King's Community Church, were never dull. His sense of humour and lack of intensity made for an easy friendship between us.

Finding an opportunity to sit down and talk about Albania for any length of time was difficult. In order to capture that elusive time we arranged to go to Rutland. Because the hotel was full we were obliged to share a twin-bedded room. During the early hours of the morning we had an intruder. A huge man, eighteen or nineteen stone I'd guess, woke us from our sleep by turning the bedroom lights on. To add to the shock, he was completely naked! He stood there, blinking disbelievingly at us. No words were exchanged: how do you start a conversation in such circumstances? Our intruder, who I assumed to be in his mid-twenties, then turned and walked into our bathroom, where he noisily emptied what must have been a large and full bladder into our toilet. He returned, looked blankly at us again, and then went out of the room into the corridor.

After a few moments, I said, 'Gary, did you just see a fat, naked man come in and use our bathroom?'

Gary confirmed that it hadn't been a vision, divine or otherwise.

After phoning the hotel reception, I peered around our door to see our nocturnal visitor in the corridor, slumped against a wall. A porter appeared with a blanket and ushered him to his room. The next morning I spotted him in reception, now fully clothed, thank goodness. Had he remembered anything of the night before?

'I got tanked up,' he said.

He had no recollection of dropping in on us . . .

* * *

Two months after my departure, news reports concerning the situation in Albania had dried up. Communications from the Albanian Encouragement Project hinted at a slight easing of tensions. Purely as a fact-finding trip, Gary and I decided to travel to nearby Corfu to gather information from people 'in the know'. When would it be safe to return? Contact by telephone with friends in Saranda and Borsh led us to make a low-key visit back into Albania. We were assured that as long as trusted Albanian friends accompanied us, we'd be quite safe.

Dutch companions Jasper and Andre travelled on the ferry with us. Also on board was a thick-set Albanian man, wearing a T-shirt bearing the somewhat disconcerting motif, 'Mad and bad, take it or leave it.' As we chugged towards Saranda Port, he gleefully pointed to a heap of concrete protruding from out of the sea. He said that it had been dumped there from a cargo boat whose captain had been taken hostage. When the terms of his release were not adhered to, the ship's load was sunk.

More reassuring was the news that a stolen gunboat and tanks had been returned to their rightful places. Jasper and Andre had already made a couple of trips to assess how their work was going during their own enforced absences. On those occasions the ferry captain had told them that it wasn't safe to stop the boat, so all the passengers had to make a jump for it as the vessel neared Saranda's quayside. We were more fortunate because our boat actually moored before disembarkation.

My friend Bujar was one of the first on board and hugged us both warmly. As we travelled by car to Borsh, where we spent two trouble free nights, our front passenger Gjergi sat with an automatic rifle resting on his lap. In the camera pouch hanging from his belt he had a concealed hand grenade. Seeing our normally passive friend armed in this way gave us a clear signal of the current state of affairs. It emerged that banditry on the roads was commonplace. In fact, with so many guns at large it was to take years to recover just a small percentage of all those looted. Law and order had been replaced for a short time by mob rule. Bujar's opinion was, 'If the lions see that you are weak, you will be attacked.'

In response, the government had devised a novel way of paying its employees and transferring essential funds during the crisis. A coffin was filled with cash, put into a hearse complete with four weeping female mourners, and then despatched to the required destination.

When we went to inspect my home, two or three bullet holes in a window were the only visible evidence of damage to the house during my long absence. Eqerem and Zuli called by and invited us for lunch. Over a plate of goat's brains, we were amused to hear that Eqerem's greatest concern during the troubles was how all the noisy gunfire had put his beloved bees off making their honey. He then went on to recall how several people had come looking for my vehicle when they heard I'd left the country.

'They tried to intimidate me into handing the keys over.'

However, he outwitted them by saying that before my departure, he'd purchased the vehicle from me and it was now his property.

Eqerem subsequently took it to a safer location, behind someone's home in Ferme. There it kept company with several chickens, a cow and a couple of pigs. In fact, it wasn't until several months later that I was finally able to recover our stricken Land Rover. Feelings had run high over the amount of money that should be paid in return for its safekeeping; whilst negotiations were in progress, a shotgun was cocked. In keeping with what briefly resembled a scene from the Wild West, an agreement was reached, *for a few dollars more*.

Before concluding that first short visit, Gary and I visited Lami and Negji, the father and mother of 18-year-old Armand. They lived in a badly constructed red brick and concrete block of flats in Ferme. Like most teenage boys at that time, Armand had become fascinated with the number of guns that were in common circulation. As he sat alone in the living room examining a pistol, he heard his mother's key in the front door. Anxious to conceal the gun from her, he hurriedly pushed the pistol down into his trouser belt and accidentally pulled the trigger. He died thirty minutes later.

Negji told us that the day before the tragedy she found a notebook in Armand's room. Beneath a drawing of a cross he had written, 'God is with me.' Because she had found a personal faith a few months earlier, she took comfort from reading what may have been the last thing her son ever wrote. On Negji's request, we prayed together. Before making the visit, we had taken advice on local customs relating to bereavements. As a token of respect, I smoked a cigarette when offered one and we left some money in the saucers of our Turkish coffee cups.

Further low-key visits to Borsh followed, but I could not return to live there before law and order had been restored. This could only happen after General Elections, which were to be held at the end of June. During the run-up to the nationwide ballot, the eventual victor – Fatos Nano of the Socialist Party – was driven through the village. I happened to be in Borsh on the day in question and was astonished when a hot-headed neighbour of mine, a supporter of the outgoing President, started firing a machine-gun at the distant cavalcade. He had also recently shot dead four donkeys because he objected to the noise they made. On this occasion, he didn't hit anybody, but got an earful from Zuli, who told him off for standing near to her home as he fired.

'We might get the blame for what you're doing,' she complained.

I spent three restless months in Corfu, helping out at the welcoming and lively English-speaking Holy Trinity Anglican Church. Along with friends Malcolm and Carol Diggens, I took language lessons from some Albanian evacuees. Malcolm had set up a car mechanics training school for young Albanian apprentices in Saranda. The 1997 uprising was the death knell for their Dutch-funded initiative because the premises they used were looted.

These were restless months because I knew that my allegiance was back in the rough and tumble of village life. I returned to my rented house in Borsh during

September of that year. Mere survival wasn't enough. I wanted to make a meaningful contribution, so that the words of our vision statement – 'to bring the positive message of the Christian faith through faith and example' – became as relevant to the child in school as to the old man tending goats on the hillside.

No matter how good my intentions were, from time to time situations came along that exposed my weakness. One such incident had arisen when I returned home at the end of a tiring day. Eqerem was standing under the open-sided concrete shelter at the top of the path where I kept the Land Rover. A group of strangers were there too, all looking down at the house. It hadn't been the best of days, and it was cold and pouring with rain. The people had no way of getting to their homes in the village of Kuç, which was an hour's drive away. Their bus had failed to return and they were stranded in Borsh. Could I take them home?

I felt irritable. I was being asked to offer a taxi service to strangers. Had they come to me because I was gaining a reputation for being the soft Englishman, who could easily be talked into helping out? I refused their offer of payment, saying that I was not there to make money. Grudgingly, I said that I would take them. The track we drove along went from bad to worse. As rain thundered down in the darkness, the absence of any form of lighting along the way made visibility poor. We twisted and bounced our way along the precarious, unsurfaced mountain road.

The windows were constantly steamed up due to the large number of people inside, and a baby was crying in the back. To make matters worse, the low fuel warning light was flashing and there seemed little prospect of finding diesel anywhere. When we eventually got to the village, a bus owner refused to give me any fuel. I felt completely helpless. I was sitting in the vehicle alone when I said a few words of prayer. You would be mistaken to think that my mood was calm and spiritually inclined. I was miserable and grumpy. An invitation to go inside the house of some of my passengers came a few minutes later, and I pompously refused to go in.

Eventually, I relented and went inside. *Raki*, coffee, Turkish delight, walnuts and cake were served as men sat in one room, women in another. In the room being occupied by the women was a wood-burning stove; the smell of damp clothes drying out hung in the air. Soon the other room had some heat in it. The rug was peeled back and a type of metal dustbin lid containing hot cinders was placed on the stone floor. For a time, an old lady dressed in customary black, came in and sat with us. She smoked a cigarette and entered into the conversation. She warmly embraced me several times before saying that I must visit them again one day. A can of fuel was produced from someone's back yard and after many kisses and handshakes we made our way outside into the wet night once more.

On the return journey, Eqerem chattered away. Maybe he genuinely liked my company, but his constant criticisms of my struggle with the confounded language left me feeling deflated. Before eventually retiring to bed, I sat at my father's battered old bureau, shipped across inside the Land Rover, writing an account of the day's events. My diary had become a close companion. I realized that I should not have considered the trip to Kuç as an unwelcome intrusion into my day. If I was to genuinely befriend my neighbours, I had to learn to take personal inconveniences in my stride. More than that; though achieving a high degree of mutual understanding may have been extremely difficult, I should do all I could to understand the people I was living alongside.

Fortunately, I was a good listener. Old black and white photographs, lovingly stored in family albums, gave me a privileged glimpse into Albania's formerly secret world. In those days, even a bus journey from Borsh to Saranda could only be made by obtaining prior permission. Such was the premium on bus tickets, the question of seat allocations often led to controversy; everyone wanted to sit at the front. To my amusement, I was told that one day the exasperated bus driver started the return journey to Borsh driving in reverse.

'There you are,' he said, 'now those of you sitting at the back have a front seat view.'

As I listened to accounts of times past, I reflected on how different our lives had been. During every year of secondary school, the pupils spent three months engaged in a combination of military training and 'action'. The military training involved gun handling, and brought with it strict discipline and order. Threat of invasion was a seed planted in every young mind. The nationwide labyrinth of tunnels and the construction of between 600,000 and 700,000 concrete bunkers reinforced the ethos of readiness for enemy attack. Because domestic telephones were a rarity, individuals were responsible for verbally alerting others in the event of an invasion.

'Action' typically meant hard physical labour – for example working in the fields or helping construct bridges. Indeed the themes of hard physical work, pitifully modest supplies of rationed food, fear of open speech, a respect for strict law and order, and a ban on any form of religious freedom were regularly referred to. To my surprise, I heard few expressions of bitterness towards former political leaders, even though many people, particularly the elderly, talked of lives lost or wasted. One day, a taxi driver told me about someone who was reported for tampering with his television aerial in order to pick up pictures from overseas. At his court trial, the prosecution witness was unable to identify where the defendant actually lived; despite that, he went to political prison for nine years.

Seclusion from the outside world was rigorously enforced. I was travelling on a bus one day when the white-haired man sitting next to me turned and started talking to me in English. After living in Australia for forty-five years, he had returned to live out his final years with his family in Himare, a seaside town about ten miles north of Borsh. He spoke of the freedom we enjoy in the western world, contrasting that with the life of Albanians pre-1991. I asked him whether he could give me an insight into what the average person thought about the brutal State he described. He told me that during those dark days feelings were not discussed, even within families. Everyone was constantly looking over his or her shoulder, for fear of the internal security services. A word out of place would lead to charges of being a spy. It was common for a young man to leave his home for work in the morning, never to return again. Fear of reprisal prevented people from asking questions about the whereabouts of missing relatives.

On another day, I heard a story that seemed to sum up this unimaginably difficult period of Albanian history. A woodcutter went into a forest to cut trees, accompanied by his donkey. Whilst there, he embarked upon an audible outburst in which he catalogued all of his grievances in life: shortage of food, low wages, and so on. Unknown to him, there was another man within earshot who stood silently amongst the trees. The eavesdropper then set off to eagerly inform the authorities of everything he'd heard. Not long after the woodcutter returned home the police arrived. He was asked to explain why he was complaining about so many things. Such indiscretions were regarded as being treacherous in those days. The woodcutter initially denied everything, but when he was accurately quoted and precise timings were given, he admitted everything. As he was led away, he added gravely, 'I never knew my donkey was such a good communist!'

Questions about life in England were occasionally asked. However, most people were more interested in telling me what they knew about my country. Many appeared to have a Dickensian view of life in England, no doubt attributable to the strictly controlled information made available to the masses during the lifespan of the regime.

It was Shako the carpenter who first introduced my palate to blackbird. He was a man who consistently showed friendship towards me, regardless of the company he was in. During one visit to his home, his wife Shaqe cooked the blackbirds Shako had shot earlier that day. The delicacy arrived on a plate with *lakra*, a wild cabbage that everyone said was good for the eyes.

'You eat everything,' Shako told me as he picked up on my dilemma as to where to start. 'Beak, legs, the lot.'

It was very tasty; later I thought about the nursery rhyme that goes, 'four and twenty blackbirds baked in a pie'. We must have eaten them ourselves back in England, in years gone by. As I crunched away, Shako asked me to give him an explanation as to why Prince Charles sometimes chose to wear a skirt.

'What he does privately at home is his own business, but to do it publicly is disgusting I think.'

I explained about kilts as best I could, but I don't think Shako was fully convinced.

There were two things I was repeatedly asked. One was to help with the granting of visas to England. I had to disappoint every person who made such a request. Of course, I did not have the authority to produce visas. One man spent ninety minutes trying to persuade me to help him as I gave him a lift from Saranda to Borsh. He even promised that if I got him his papers, he would replace the icon hung on his bedroom wall with my photograph and then pray to it every night!

Travel restrictions continue to be a bone of contention to this day. By comparison, my own freedom to come and go as I pleased gave further evidence of the differences between the villagers and myself. During the time when I was preparing to take up residency in Albania, I visited Pavli Qesku, the Albanian Ambassador in London. When asked what visas or travel permits were required to live in his country, he said that all I needed was my passport: 'We say that if you have a British passport you have the keys to paradise.'

The other popular request was to teach English to the village children. In a country that had so many needs, I had at times become demoralized by thinking of all the things I wasn't able to do. Now I was being presented with an opportunity to make a useful contribution by simply using my mother tongue. Despite reservations and a lack of teaching experience, I felt that I should at least give it a go. I could try to equip some of the children with a marketable skill: the ability to communicate in English. Even though my sending church did not have a big missions budget from which I could draw, this wasn't a problem: the costs involved would be negligible.

I went to ask the local director of education, Shuapi, for permission to use the school premises after lessons had finished. I naïvely thought that this would be a formality, but he refused my request. He did subsequently change his mind, possibly due to pressure applied by keen parents.

He told me with a smile, 'You can start whenever you like.'

I was free to use any of the three schools situated within Borsh's boundaries. Before taking Shuapi up on his offer, I conducted one or two pilot lessons with neighbours' children.

As I approached the three-storey secondary school for my first lesson, I was heartily greeted by several boys who were running about on the flat roof. The building was devoid of all modern educational equipment; in fact it lacked almost any form of equipment – educational or otherwise. Inside, the classrooms were old-fashioned wooden bench desks and worn blackboards, but little else. Glass was missing from several of the window frames. Forty youngsters tried squeezing into the thirty seats available in the room I was to use. I had to ask several to leave, but assured them that they would be able to come and learn at a different time. Five minutes into the lesson, a brick came crashing through one of the windows, showering us all in glass. I rushed downstairs to find the culprit. It was a blonde-haired, blue-eyed little girl, one of those I'd asked to come back another time. Evidently she did not think much of my offer.

The following week, no one had a key to get into the school so we had to enter the classroom via an empty window frame. I had to prepare well for the lessons because I needed to have everything I taught covered in Albanian as well as in English. I can't say that I really enjoyed those lessons; they were something to survive rather than enjoy.

Even though there were challenges, my times of teaching in the schools gave me some precious memories. Little boys really do still make paper aeroplanes during lessons, and some come away with Biro marks on their foreheads thanks to the efforts of fellow classmates.

Sometimes it was hard to keep a straight face when the boys came to ask me about the meanings of various English swear words they'd picked up from dubbed American films they'd watched at home.

I usually walked home after lessons with something to smile about. During one Friday session in Shkalle, after learning the names for members of the family, one young boy asked me if I was married. When I told him that I wasn't, he responded by saying, 'How many lovers do you have then?' Another afternoon in Ferme, I arrived to find all the children waiting outside the school building.

'We're waiting for the cleaner to finish,' someone said.

After five minutes or so, an 8-year-old girl called Dushe came out with a sweeping brush taller than her: she was the cleaner.

The most unusual incident came after I'd had to throw the headmaster's son, Tini, out of the classroom for bad behaviour. Ten minutes after, there was a knock on the classroom door. I went to open it, ready to give a telling off to whoever was there. To my amazement, a donkey was standing there. Tini had led it up the three flights of stairs. I couldn't maintain my serious expression and we all laughed when I said that the donkey couldn't stay because it hadn't brought a notebook and pen.

Although I was usually able to maintain an acceptable level of discipline during lessons, I was to eventually realize that many of the youngsters attending my classes had no true enthusiasm to learn. Instead, I started teaching those with a genuine desire to learn English, in their homes. One of these was 10-year-old Eldion, who used an upturned oil drum covered with a piece of plastic as a desk. This transition was a decisive and positive step in building good relations with extended family circles. It was important to always honour those teaching appointments. My young pupils and their parents often expressed grateful surprise when I arrived in bad weather, carrying my whiteboard and bag of pens under my arm. I wanted them to know that I could be depended on.

As my integration into the village gained momentum, other things, some of them particularly significant, had been happening elsewhere. During the days of our first team visits to Borsh, 28-year-old German-born Kristin had been one of our translators. She had been working for a missionary organization called Operation Mobilization, in Albania's second city Durres, for four years. She liked the look of our mission outreach in Borsh and so a period of induction was set up after talking with Gary back in England. This involved her working in our Bedworth church office for a time. By spring of 1998, she had joined the mission full time, and had moved in with my neighbours, Muqo and Tonja. Kristin's responsibility was to develop the work in the neighbourhoods of Ferme and Shkalle. Shortly after arriving, she was invited to a female neighbour's home for coffee. Kristin later told me that even though she was amongst relative strangers, she felt at ease. In fact, she felt more at home in Borsh than in any other place she'd ever been to.

5

DIFFICULT DAYS

Walking from one neighbourhood to the next gave me lots of thinking time, maybe too much. How was I doing? Where had I been? Where was I going? The fear of being considered a failure – particularly in the eyes of others, rightly or wrongly, weighed heavily on my mind. Some things were going well, others more slowly. The bridge-building element of the work was inching forward. Overcoming a natural shyness, as well as the occasional dish of unusual food, were small prices to pay in reaching an important goal. But what of the spiritual content of our work? Although much of it was hard to quantify, I mentally carried an image of my head banging against granite-like Borsh rocks. Something tangible, such as a regular gathering of new believers would represent considerable progress.

Little, if any, pressure was applied from outside. The pressure came from within: I wanted to deliver the goods, win my stripes and honour the gamble people had taken on me. The battle with worldly pride apart, there was still much ground to cover. I passionately wanted to succeed, or at least not to fail. Kristin's presence helped move the level of communications up several notches. Her excellent command of the Albanian language meant that when engaged in conversation we could attempt to give specific definitions and answers.

A good example of the type of situation I'm referring to was found at the home of Anna and her husband Gjika. They lived in Ferme, behind a high wall with a green metal door in it. Outside, ducks quacked about in the large puddles on the muddy road. Kristin and I visited each week. 'Come as often as you like,' they said. Our hosts were in their late twenties and had two children, one of whom was only a few months old.

Anna was very slim, with long, straight hair, which she usually swept back. Gjika had one of the hairiest chests I've ever seen. Tufts of thick growth protruded from his collar line. How did he know where to stop shaving? Anna and Gjika were genuinely on a spiritual search. Fortunately, we were usually able to satisfy their many questions.

'If you're a Christian, are you allowed to celebrate birthdays?'

'What makes Christianity different from Islam?'

'Do you really believe Jesus rose from the dead?'

Kristin and I were careful with our answers. We didn't incorporate a cultural slant on things and sought to make our answers biblically based. As the nature of the discussion was always good-humoured, some of their neighbours heard about it and started attending. They included Nedo, an elderly friend who'd sit with her knitting as we talked.

In Shkalle a similar meeting took place at Profi and Eftelira's home. They were both pensioners; Eftelira was blind. We were alerted to their need for spiritual support on our first introductions. An upstairs neighbour, renowned for dabbling in dark spiritual practices, had been disturbing them. Having lost a grown son in tragic circumstances, she was jealous of Profi and Eftelira's wage-earning children who lived in Greece.

Profi and Eftelira were frightened, describing physical manifestations of the curses placed on them. Our prayers and invitation to explore John's gospel every Thursday morning were well-received. Kristin made the Turkish coffee, in line with the traditional view of what men did or didn't do in the home. In the winter months when the Land Rover was out of action, we would often walk through rain for forty-five minutes each way. Their flat was always cold, so our wet clothes never dried out.

I suppose both gatherings could be described as 'church meetings', so for a time I became less anxious regarding the success syndrome. In the end, both couples, like hundreds of others, emigrated to Greece in hope of a new and better life.

My own spiritual journey continued. On 12 May 1998, I was baptized. This came relatively late for me as a believer: my church life pre-Albania didn't involve adult water baptisms. The symbolism of baptism was important, having reached a place where I wanted to separate certain aspects of my old life from the new. Jeremy Parkes took the service back in Dudley, West Midlands. Afterwards he gave me a card that read, 'Upon confession of faith in Jesus Christ as Saviour and Lord, Richard Welch was baptized in the name of God the Father, God the Son and God the Holy Spirit.'

My prayer life developed with the move to Albania. A thirty-six-hour fast became a weekly discipline for me. I continually sought direction about what my personal attitude and subsequent actions should be based upon. The message came loud and clear: I was to serve the people. Patience, endurance and stamina were required in large doses. I got ample opportunity to put this into practice during a ten-week period that stretched me in a way I'd never experienced before. Like distant rumbles of thunder, trouble was brewing in Kosovo.

Kosovo is a semi-autonomous mountainous region of south-west Serbia. It borders north-eastern Albania. But

Kosovo's rich, fertile valleys, combined with a very different modern political history, have provided its citizens with a more affluent lifestyle. I say semi-autonomous as, once part of Albania, when its borders were redefined in 1913 it became Serbian territory. Yugoslav President Tito had given Kosovo autonomy, but this was rescinded in 1989 by President Milosevic.

Kosovo's most famous daughter, Gonxhe Bojaxhi was born in 1902. She went on to receive the Nobel peace prize and at the presentation ceremony said, 'I always keep my Albanian people in my heart and I pray to God that his peace and love be in our hearts, in every home.' We know her better as Mother Teresa.

In March 1998, fifty Kosovar Albanians were killed when Serbian forces sealed off a village. A programme of ethnic cleansing had begun. What followed was a ruthlessly executed, cold-blooded genocide. NATO's involvement in resolving the problem stemmed the flow of violence in December 1998. Serbian assaults recommenced sporadically, either side of peace talks in Paris, in February 1999.

* * *

Yvonne Perry and Joanne Simpson, from Bedworth and West Bromwich respectively, had a visit to Borsh scheduled in the early spring of 1999. Yvonne co-ordinated much of our administrative work back in England. Joanne wanted to take another look at life in Albania, with a view to joining the mission full-time. After escorting them down to Borsh, we spent several fruitful days together, and Joanne's progression towards joining Kristin and I continued to gain momentum. In order to make their return flights to England, I drove Joanne and Yvonne back up to the capital.

At that time, travelling without Albanian friends was still considered unsafe, so Bujar, always willing to make a trip to Tirana, jumped at the chance when it was time to make our way back up to the capital. This ensured that I wouldn't have to make the return journey alone. Thinking that I'd be driving back to Borsh with Bujar as my only passenger, I readily agreed to transport some furniture for him. The coastal guesthouse he was building with his brothers needed basic furniture and Tirana's prices were significantly lower than in the south.

We had time to kill in Tirana because the scheduled flight to England was the following day. As Joanne, Yvonne and I walked along a crowded street, we stopped to join dozens of others looking skywards. We saw vapour trails behind a group of barely visible jets, flying in formation, high above the wispy clouds. A voice from the crowd said, 'NATO'. Word quickly spread that Tirana Airport had been closed. All commercial flights, including those to England had been cancelled. NATO was about to start bombing strategic Serbian targets and insisted on exclusive control of airspace. As the evening progressed, we heard rumours that the seaports throughout Albania had also been closed. Apparently, measures were being taken to stop Serbian agitators entering Albania.

Early the next day, I made a visit to Stephen Nash, the British Ambassador in Tirana. The armed guard on duty let me pass after examining my passport and obtaining clearance over an intercom system. The Ambassador, wearing slippers, greeted me in the hallway of his home. A welcome aroma of bacon cooking wafted through from another part of the house. Unfortunately a waft was all that came my way. The Ambassador reported that currently there was no reason for British citizens to leave Albania, even as a precautionary measure. He hadn't heard the rumours concerning port closures, but allowed me to use his telephone to contact the British Consulate in Corfu. I was pleased to hear that the ferry between Saranda and Corfu was operating normally, as was the airport.

Having developed a good working relationship with Allways Travel Agency in Corfu, I quickly arranged alternative flights from Corfu to England for Joanne and Yvonne. This meant that we had to return to Borsh. Four other English people from a church in Milton Keynes were to accompany them.

The drive back to Borsh had elements of comedy about it.

'I've already agreed to transport some furniture for a friend, so it'll be a bit of a squeeze,' I told my six English friends.

With Bujar included, I was carrying seven passengers, two tables, sixteen chairs and four chickens. Fortunately I had a roof rack. Rain lashed down as darkness fell, but our spirits were kept high by the sound of chickens clucking in the darkness. They didn't seem to mind the squash; in fact they made themselves so comfortable that they laid a few eggs during the journey. Bujar mischievously asked me what my associates thought of life in Albania. After spending the night at our base house I bid our friends farewell at Saranda Port.

The rumbles got louder. A spokesman from NATO talked of a pending humanitarian catastrophe as Serbian paramilitary police began firing indiscriminately in ethnic Albanian villages. Their aggressors typically gave Albanian families five minutes to pack up and leave. Newspapers and television showed pictures of a seemingly endless line of wretched-looking individuals, pouring across the Albanian border. Some of them were driving tractors; others were so desperate to get out that they drove cars that had no tyres, but the majority were on foot.

The first rescue station was the town of Kukes. Inevitably, the sheer volume of people cramming into a limited space caused overcrowding; something had to give. Albania's government decreed that it was necessary to spread the burden of refugee care all across the country. Waves of buses arrived in practically every town and large village. I called in at the Lidia Foundation offices in Saranda. A Dutch funded humanitarian aid organization, I was sure they would be involved in the refugee support effort. I offered accommodation for up to twelve refugees at our base house.

Along a scenic stretch of Saranda's shoreline is a big square concrete building, referred to as 'The Workers' Camp'. The derelict property, with overgrown gardens, had once provided holiday accommodation for the chosen few during Albania's years in isolation. Six hundred refugees inhabited it, sharing four toilets and two showers. I felt uncomfortable knowing that refugees were pouring into my nearest town, whilst I was living alone in a property that would comfortably accommodate twelve people. It wasn't long before I became involved in the efforts to give shelter and temporary relief to the Kosovars.

To make a direct comparison between Local Authorities in Britain and those in Albania would be wildly inaccurate. My personal experience of Albanian bureaucracy is that it is old-fashioned and cumbersome. It's a dinosaur when compared to the relatively fast-moving, technologically driven operation back home. For the sake of convenience, however, I will refer to the bureaucrats governing the zone incorporating Borsh as being the 'Local Authority'. It became apparent that Borsh would receive a quota of refugees. Information was understandably difficult to come by, in what was a period of crisis for the entire country.

Some political commentators said that Serbia's President Milosevic was not just trying to destabilize Kosovo, but the whole of Albania. Barely able to support its own people under normal circumstances, Albania was doing its valiant best for the misplaced. The dilemma for Prime Minister Majko was how to provide for the 20,000 refugees a day that were crossing the border into Albania. With a peacetime population of just under 3.5 million, 600,000 refugees poured into the country. I became anxious when word reached me that my village's Local Authority thought that I would personally shoulder most of the responsibility for up to five hundred refugees.

It wasn't a time for burying my head in the sand, but neither did I have the resources to meet the approaching tidal wave of need. It is rare for me not to sleep well. However, as the once-distant rumbles crept up closer, sleep became more elusive. My efforts to win the trust and confidence of the villagers may have gone too well. Could I take the matter of finding accommodation, water, electricity, food, blankets and access to reliable medical care for up to five hundred people easily in my stride? For sure I would do everything I could to help, but others would have to help work the pump too.

The civil service job I was doing prior to emigrating was managing industrial relations. Although it never happened, my biggest professional dread was that the staff would walk out over an act of negligence on my part. In those days I would have viewed two hundred staff standing in the office car parks as a real crisis. Now, as I lay in my bed, my stomach turned over like a washing machine on a short wash. The prospect of being personally responsible for several hundred refugees

gave me a deeper understanding of what the word 'crisis' could mean.

Bujar had a brother, Sihat, who had Local Authority
connections. Because he spoke English, I was able to con-
verse in my mother tongue. I'd envisioned going to
Corfu to obtain essential aid supplies. However, getting
them through Albanian customs would be problematic.
Sihat, a former customs officer, was reassuring. He'd
been instructed to arrange a meeting between senior
Local Authority personnel and myself, with a view to
discussing the imminent arrival of refugees.

Sihat and I waited for our meeting to begin as we sat
at a table in a café in Borsh's centre. The tablecloth had
many cigarette burns in it. Eventually the men we were
waiting for turned up; they didn't join us at our table,
but found seats on the other side of the café. Their mood
seemed light, as though they didn't have a care in the
world. After several minutes of waiting, Sihat said, 'We
should go; if they can't be bothered to talk to us, why
should we sit here wasting our time?'

Shortly after reaching Sihat's home, the Local
Authority men arrived. Sihat fired a verbal volley their
way and they listened to his expletives without flinch-
ing. After the inevitable round of handshakes we sat
down together. I had to be clear on what I could and
couldn't do. The Local Authority was to assume overall
responsibility for the refugees. My role would be to supply blankets, cookers, any clothing I could get my hands
on, and maybe help with miscellaneous expenses.
Albania's central government would supply basic foodstuffs, obtainable on production of official vouchers.

As I drove home after the meeting through the village
centre, I was stopped at a police checkpoint. Alongside it
was a corrugated iron hut that housed a makeshift bed.
Usually a friendly wave of the hand to a familiar man in

uniform meant I didn't even have to stop. Tonight it was different. A man in his late twenties, dressed in plain clothes, flashed his ID at me. His manner was brusque and formal. Without being invited, he opened the passenger door and got in. I hadn't met him before and there was no hint of courtesy in his voice as he instructed me to drive some forty yards up the road. There we would be out of earshot of the other policemen at the checkpoint.

'Turn the engine off,' he said curtly. 'Who are you and where do you live?'

I answered his questions and then he said, 'What other houses do you have?'

I replied, 'I don't have any other houses.'

He coldly repeated the same question several times. I couldn't understand what was at the root of his questions.

He continued, 'Who were the two women that stayed at your house recently?'

Although Joanne and Yvonne didn't actually sleep at the base house, they had spent time there. I explained that the two women were friends from a church in England.

A chill ran down my spine at the thought of an apparently friendly neighbour privately informing the authorities of Joanne and Yvonne's trip. Who could it have been? The questions continued.

'What's the currency in England? How much money do you have in your pockets? Empty them now.'

I thought to myself, 'This is bizarre,' as I found myself bearing the contents of my pockets to the hostile stranger: a few coins, a couple of notes, a house key, a grubby tissue and a ball of used chewing gum within a screwed up sweet wrapper.

'I know what you do, and God knows what you do,' he continued.

'And what do you think that is?'

'You know,' he said.

I had absolutely no idea what he was getting at. My Albanian hadn't reached the level of 'You're barking up the wrong tree.' The interrogation lasted twenty minutes. At times he went quiet on me. He continued staring and began to tap one of his feet on the dusty floor of the vehicle.

'You're a liar,' he said rudely.

'Thank you,' I said, not flippantly, but to show that he did not intimidate me.

The same questions were repeated, but in different ways: 'I have been trained in psychology and when I look into your eyes I see a liar.' It went on. After we had gone round in a few more circles he wound up the exchange.

'We will meet again, but next time it will be more serious for you, not like this time. Do you understand me?'

I can't say I understood every word he spoke, but I was left in no doubt that he was trying to frighten me.

'Yes, I understand you,' I said.

'What do I mean, then?' His voice now slightly raised.

'You mean next time we meet it will mean this.'

At that point I held my right hand to look like a gun.

'Bang, Bang,' I said.

'Yes,' he responded, then continued, 'you should go to prison for eight years for what you are doing.'

Although this had been the most sinister exchange I'd ever had with an Albanian, it actually ended remarkably politely. He shook my hand and wished me good night. When he got out of the Land Rover I had the presence of mind to check his name. As I drove back down the road near to the roadblock, I saw him getting into an unmarked white Mercedes. I noted the registration number, pulling over to scribble it down on a scrap of paper.

I was going to make my own investigations into who he was.

I told several friends in the village about my encounter with the sinister policeman. I thought that certain friends, who had some standing and influence, would be able to tap into the underground network of communications. During the following few days, word reached me that the man in question worked for the secret police. I had little to worry about, however, because people in the village had spoken up for me. Some people spoke of me as being like a brother or son to them. Even if those words had been used lightly, I was still grateful to hear of their acceptance of me and felt all the safer because of them.

I did not encounter further problems with the secret policeman, although I did see him a couple of weeks later.

He approached me to say, 'I hear you've told people that I'm a bad boy.'

I dropped a dead bat on things and we finished our conversation relatively amicably. All of this had come at a time when I was bracing myself for the arrival of the refugees. On the scale of things, I considered this to be far weightier than the personal threats I'd received from the sinister official.

Kristin and I had prayed about it together and there were prayerful people committed to our mission back home in England. However, the incident had a damaging impact on my relationship with Kristin. I failed to convince her that our prayers were sufficient and that we should now put the matter behind us. Life had to go on and there were bigger battles to fight. However, in some aspects, our defences had been breached. We spent a lot of time talking it through, but sadly I didn't find the right words or actions to kill the issue totally.

I was to encounter a further problem with the police that proved to be more insulting and provocative than sinister. During the time the refugees were staying locally, some policemen who lived in the area took a keen interest in all the fetching and carrying I was involved in. One day I was pulled over by one of them. Were any of the Kosovar women performing sexual favours for me in return for the support I was giving? His smirking expression was clearly a provocation but I resisted the bait.

Despite these two negative experiences, my general experiences of policemen in Albania had been positive. I thought they had a difficult job to do against a backdrop of an evolving organized crime network. Drug production and export, together with women trafficking, were often mentioned on the Albanian news programmes I occasionally saw at Eqerem's home. A policeman's salary of under a hundred dollars a month was peanuts in comparison to what many teenage boys made through crime, let alone those who co-ordinated it.

I would often be stopped on the road by police whilst driving outside of Borsh. My Albanian number plates gave no clue as to my foreign identity. As soon as I stopped and the officers on duty saw that I was a foreigner, I'd be given a friendly handshake and told to move on. Getting the documents for my Land Rover showed me what a maze bureaucracy can be. One paper was stamped and signed on an obliging policeman's lounge table one wet night, over a glass of *raki*.

On a different night, the Land Rover broke down just outside Borsh. A policeman, whom I didn't know, was travelling in the opposite direction to me. He stopped and asked if I needed help. I'm no mechanic, but told him that I thought the fuel pump was playing up. Without fuss, he shone his car headlights towards the front of the Land Rover and tried to make a repair. It was a bitterly cold night, and as he worked his shirt came out of his trousers at the back, exposing the small of his back to the elements.

He couldn't fix it, so offered to tow it to somewhere safe in Borsh for the night. Unfortunately he was low on diesel for his battered old Mercedes. Between us we made a funnel and found some hosepipe so that he could transfer diesel from my vehicle into his. To start the required flow, he had to suck through the pipe, getting a mouthful of diesel in the process. He then towed me safely home. The policeman, Ardian, an imposing-looking man from the village of Shenvasil, wished me well before driving off into the night. I was truly impressed by his attitude; he'd been a tremendous ambassador for the Albanian police force.

I became increasingly immersed in the refugee situation. The Local Authority, via Sihat, told me that up to five hundred refugees would be heading for Borsh. I wanted to telephone International Rescue, but for once 'Thunderbirds weren't go'. They were inexplicably out of range, so I needed to find help elsewhere. Telephone discussions with contacts back in England threw up the name of an English church charity that operated in Lexhe, a town north of Tirana. I established contact with the co-ordinator who told me that I could have three hundred blankets.

Sihat accompanied me on the journey to Lexhe. There we met some Kosovars who'd been given sanctuary at the charity's well-run centre. I gave a lift to some refugees who were staying in a different part of town, but on my way back to where Sihat and I were staying, I took a wrong turning. I realized my mistake almost immediately and turned the Land Rover round in the road. Fifty yards or so further down the road was a parked police van. The sight of me turning round, possibly to avoid a confrontation rang an alarm bell with the policemen. Their vehicle roared past and pulled up across my path. Several armed policemen jumped out, all wearing combat gear. They trained their guns on me as one man approached my window. As soon as he realized that I was an Englishman his manner lightened considerably. He gave me instructions to find my way back to where I was staying and wished me well.

Before setting off on the twelve-hour drive back to Borsh the following morning, the Land Rover bulging with blankets, Sihat decided he wanted a photograph taken with the Kosovar men he'd delighted in meeting. He gave them every encouragement to endure this time of suffering. Once home I set about carrying the blankets down the steep track to my home, where I would store them temporarily. To my amazement a neighbour and his wife came out and asked if they could exchange some of their older blankets for newer ones. I refused this request. The people in question weren't poor; they had family working over in Greece and regularly received money from them. Their jealousy had echoes elsewhere in the village. At times I found the balance between looking after the refugees and continuing to honour my commitment to the villagers a difficult one to achieve. Partly to demonstrate my loyalty to the people of Borsh, I continued teaching English throughout the crisis period. I didn't want to drop my normal day-to-day commitments, if at all possible, in order to serve a different set of needy people.

The day after delivering the first batch of blankets to Borsh I was on the road again. I'd been offered more essential provisions by the charity working in Lexhe. A fleet of lorries packed full of aid were coming from Manchester, England. Several days later, I returned home, followed by one of the lorries. During the hot, dusty journey I reflected on what a hard-nosed operation humanitarian aid work could be. I had become caught in the crossfire of an angry confrontation between the arriving English lorry drivers and the waiting aid workers. Much to the interest of a documentary-making English TV crew, tempers had frayed as insults were traded back and forth. I was appreciative of the supplies, but glad to get on my way again. The English lorry driver, whose entire load had been consigned to me, had been given an Albanian travelling companion. Every time we stopped, for diesel or to answer the call of nature behind a convenient bush, the likeable Albanian gave me a chocolate fix. From somewhere he had got hold of a box of Fry's Turkish Delight bars.

I took the unusual step of driving at night until we reached Gjirokaster, about two and a half hours away from Borsh. Road travel still couldn't be done with complete confidence, especially at night. As if to demonstrate the point, as I turned a corner I was confronted by several men standing in the road. They were carrying machine-guns and wore balaclavas covering their faces. My blood ran cold as one of the armed men stepped forward to my stationary vehicle.

'I'm carrying aid,' I told the man.

I breathed a sigh of relief as he nodded and waved me on. Shortly afterwards we stopped for a few hours rest in a lorry park. At first light we completed the final stretch of the journey.

At Lukove, where the Local Authority was based, I'd made arrangements for a store to be set up in the school. The local officials enthusiastically signed for the twenty-two cubic metres of clothes, twenty-two cubic metres of blankets, three boxes of soap, three boxes of disinfectant and forty boxes of toiletries that I entrusted into their care.

When I got to Borsh, it felt good to wash and shave for the first time in four days. After a welcome change of clothes, I drove down to the site of what had once been a children's home. Derelict for many years, it was housing the first of the Kosovo refugees to arrive. I'd walked past the two-storey building hundreds of times, but hadn't ever closely inspected it. A rusty gate was still in place, open wide enough for the occasional roaming cow to enter and take shelter inside from the elements.

Opaque plastic sheets had been fixed over the window frames and there were lots of people milling about. The Local Authority had sanctioned the use of these premises, which at least provided basic shelter. Inside I met a person called Tahir. A thickset man in his late fifties, he had a ruddy complexion and short-cropped hair. When I introduced myself he smiled and said, 'I know who you are.' By observing several friendly exchanges between Tahir and some of his fellow refugees, it was evident that he was their leader and spokesperson. With the exception of the sounds of their words, which were strange to me, there seemed little difference between them and the average Albanian. One of the men was wearing a type of hat that I'd never seen before. It was beige, flat-topped and made from felt. I was to later learn that it was called a *qylaf*.

Inside the various rooms, the occupants had organized themselves into extended family groups. The first consignment of blankets was very much in evidence, lying on the concrete floors. Stark walls and the complete absence of furniture created a sterile environment. What few clothes they had were piled neatly on the floor. They had a little food but nothing to cook on. The cast iron gas burners, together with the gas bottles on order from Corfu, were going to be very useful.

Talk of up to five hundred Kosovars coming to Borsh was, in the event, an exaggeration. Tahir's group was one of three to take up temporary residence in the village. A second group moved into the disused hospital. Others, who had a little money, moved into rooms used occasionally by summertime holidaymakers. Just under one hundred and eighty people arrived by bus. In nearby Piqeras two groups of refugees arrived. They were housed in several deserted flats and an old disused house. All of them were incorporated into our support programme. Each group appointed one spokesperson to receive and pass on information. The circumstances may have been unusual and I lacked experience, but listing the things I knew I could do, and then getting on with it, seemed to work well.

The day after my first meeting with Tahir I travelled to Corfu. Were the gas bottles and burners now ready? Unfortunately they were not. I withdrew all the money I had in the bank to help meet running costs. This was to be reimbursed at a future date, as the collection of emergency aid money got under way back home. Jeremy Parkes contacted my old secondary school, Ellowes Hall, in Dudley. Despite not having had any contact with the school for twenty-six years, the response was positive. Each pupil paid £1 for a non-uniform day.

Still in Corfu, I was told that Holy Trinity Church had also been collecting for the refugee aid effort. There was also a special personal gift waiting for me: a chocolate cake with a note attached. On it the words of Joshua 1:9 were written, 'Have I not commanded you? Be strong and courageous. Do not be terrified; do not be discouraged, for the LORD your God will be with you wherever you go.' I'm not sure which I enjoyed the most, the cake or the Scripture; they both went down well.

On my return from Corfu I had the first of the year's visiting teams from England with me. Marilyn, Georgina and Elaine made up a prayer group. Our visitors were able to reach out to the female Kosovars in a unique way. Reports coming out of some of their home villages were harrowing. Stories were being circulated of Serbian forces rounding up and executing large groups of Kosovar men. Many of the women hadn't received word as to the well-being of husbands, brothers or sons for many weeks.

With Kristin acting as translator, our English guests responded with compassion. They had brought toiletries with them from England that were well-received by the women living in such an austere environment. Our hearts were deeply stirred when the refugees served us sweet, black Russian tea. On 8 May 1999, my boat literally came in, something I had been expecting for a while. Now the groups of refugees had decent cooking facilities. In addition to warm bedding and hot food, I was able to continue distributing small amounts of money to every family. This enabled them to purchase necessary items as their needs arose. I was conscious of the need to give the refugees as much respect and dignity as possible. I didn't feel that being 'the man with the money bag' enhanced that objective. I wanted to think of an alternative way to distribute the money, one in which their self-esteem would not be undermined.

The religious tradition of the Kosovars is Muslim. Their adversaries back home, the people who had brutally attacked, raped and committed murder, shamefully did so under a Christian banner. I felt it necessary to reach out to the refugees spiritually as well as physically. On 15 May 1999, we stood together to observe a minute's silence out of respect for the dead and missing. Our prayer and carefully chosen Scripture from Genesis, was readily accepted.

By now early summer temperatures were starting to rise. The people living in the former children's home had to endure poor sanitary conditions. Although they had access to clean running water, I feared that the onset of an Albanian summer could bring with it an epidemic if sanitation didn't improve. I had learnt by now that Tahir and the six or so men in his group were, like all Albanians, resourceful. With the money to purchase new pipes, taps and plumbing accessories, they made short work of improving the water supply. This proved to be a major step forward, as did the eventual installation of reliable electrical lighting. Communal cooking was working out well and I kept a spanner handy for changing gas bottles in our hard-working Land Rover. Regular trips to Saranda to purchase new gas bottles also became occasions to escort people requiring medical attention to the town's hospital.

Any recollection of those days would be incomplete without paying tribute to the Catholic nuns based in Saranda. Few in number, their attitude radiated generosity and compassion whenever I approached them for help. They had a good supply line from Italy and were ever willing to share whatever was in their storeroom. Nappies, sanitary items and shoes were amongst the provisions they donated to the Borsh effort.

Further English teams came – friends from partner churches, who enthusiastically got stuck into doing whatever they could to help out. Before May was through, I had a good idea. I approached Tahir, along with the other leaders. Would the able-bodied men like to work? Receipt of a wage would eliminate the need for my cash handouts. The work would involve repairing the much used, badly maintained road that ran from Ferme through the orchard and along the coastal stretch down to the old prison. This would not only benefit the

Kosovars, who were getting bored and restless, it would also be to the advantage of the people of Borsh, since the road was important to them. The proposal was accepted and worked well. Sihat agreed to be the foreman, organizing the men and arranging for the delivery of raw materials. Stones from the semi-dried up riverbed and hard drying clay from the side of a nearby mountain road were used.

When British forces entered Prishtina, Kosovo, on 14 June 1999, the liberated Kosovars threw flowers in their path. Peace was within reach. During their stay in Borsh I can't say that the refugees ever thought of anything other than returning home as soon as possible. Some of the local people, but by no means all, treated them with disdain throughout. One woman even sabotaged the water supply of those taking shelter in the disused hospital.

One miserable afternoon, a man laid into me regarding the money I was wasting on the road repairs project. He had his own ideas on how the job could be done better, but it didn't involve deploying the Kosovars. However, the majority of the villagers sympathized with their plight. People such as retired teacher Muho and his wife Shpresa, a nurse, regularly welcomed many of the refugees to their home for coffee. For others, Sihat and Bujar's home became a regular haunt. Finding a vacant seat in front of their television set was difficult during news bulletins.

Towards the end of their stay, temperatures had reached the high thirties. 'Can you get us any sun cream?' I was occasionally asked. However, their time in Borsh didn't evolve into some sort of a holiday. Their experiences had been most traumatic. One woman in her late twenties did not know the fate of her missing husband. She lost all her hair and took to wearing a headscarf. There was little we could do about that: the reliable medical advice assured us that her hair would grow back as she became less traumatized.

As June drew to a close the refugees departed. They returned to Kosovo under the protection of an international peacekeeping force. We were able to supply them with money to meet their travelling expenses and expressed our hope to one day meet again. As their buses began the long journey back to Kosovo, some of the local men entered the premises the refugees had lodged in, and trashed whatever they could. A friend came to warn me that I should keep a low profile for a few days in order to avoid a jealous backlash that might come my way. In the event nothing more serious came than a general ten-day power cut.

During the weeks of the refugee crisis, my eyes had been frequently drawn towards the slopes of the mountains that dominate the Borsh skyline. I had consistently prayed for guidance as I negotiated situations that had the capacity to overwhelm me. Now that the storm had passed, my eyes returned to those familiar heights. I thanked the Good Shepherd for watching over me: throughout it all, I'd never been out of his reach.

6

HELPING HANDS

One still evening, long after the world's news cameras had moved away from Albania, I was invited to a night out. With the exception of an occasional supper invitation, nightlife was practically non-existent. For most villagers, the average day started at first light, when the goats were sent up into the mountains. The day ended when they returned, shortly before the sun went down.

The reason for the night out was to celebrate the agreement reached between the residents of Ferme and the local Land Commission. The prickly issue of land transference had been successfully negotiated. To commemorate the event, it had been decided that each family should pay a small contribution into a kitty that would cover the cost of food and a modest quantity of beer. I was instructed to be at Xhavo's café for 5 p.m. I felt a sense of apprehension mixed with curiosity.

When I arrived, about forty men were standing around outside in small huddles. The café, with smoked glass windows and an elegant tiled floor, was on ground level. Upstairs, bare concrete columns made up the skeleton of the construction. I was immediately introduced to the local MP from Saranda, followed by two regional dignitaries from the controlling socialist party. Much of their business seemed to be conducted in smoky bars. Nepotism, granting of favours and the acceptance of bribes was said to be the way of things.

As we shook hands, I felt a little wary of them, but at least they were polite and courteous. By contrast, the ready smiles and good humour of the local men, as we exchanged greetings, felt genuine. We were all standing around when Luman, the neighbourhood leader, asked the guests of honour – me included – to go inside for a cup of coffee. Final preparations were still being made as we went inside. I didn't feel entirely comfortable leaving all the others (by now about seventy of them) standing outside. On the one hand I had to be gracious in accepting the treatment being given to me; on the other it didn't seem proper that men who'd endured the worst of Hoxha's regime should be left standing there, whilst I was ushered in ahead of them.

Surely after surviving such a brutal dictatorship, with all of its injustices and hardships, these men deserved to be honoured ahead of me. My own life by comparison had been comfortable and one of privileges. This was their night; it was their struggle that was being reflected upon and as far as land ownership was concerned, it was their triumph. As the night wore on, however, they made it very clear that they wanted me to enjoy being a part of it.

Ten minutes later, Xhavo pronounced everything ready. Everyone crowded into the room and took their places at tables that were arranged in the shape of a big 'E'. Each setting had a can of beer placed alongside the fork, which was to be used for eating the plate of salad, followed by huge portions of goat meat. The tough old man who sat opposite me was in his seventies. He shook my hand so firmly that I felt it was part greeting, part demonstration of physical prowess. He had a grey, whiskery chin and warm eyes. As he sat down he reached into his right hand jacket pocket and pulled out a 1.5 pint bottle of homemade *raki*. He placed it on the table between us with a look that said, 'We're going to enjoy ourselves tonight.' As I looked around the room I could see that he wasn't the only one to have had that idea.

The windows were soon steamed up and the air thick and smoky. Toasts were offered and received, always with a short speech attached. One of the village elders stood up to say a few words about me, something I found to be very moving. Along with tributes to the men who served on the Land Commission, thanks were being expressed for what we were doing also. Our different activities were mentioned and I felt that this signified a growing awareness of why we were there. I was expected to make a response minutes later. In the few moments available, I scribbled some words on the paper tablecloth in front of me.

When I stood up the man sitting to my immediate left tapped his plate with a fork and asked for the music being played from a cassette recorder on the bar, to be turned down. I thanked them for their invitation and hospitality. To be part of such a special event was an honour I would not forget. I wished them well in a new chapter of their lives, as property owners. It is in unity that our strength was to be found, and the togetherness of the evening was something special. Jesus had stressed the importance of his commandment to 'Love one another.' Our purpose for being there was to love and serve their community. I concluded by thanking them for the love they showed me in my day-to-day life in Borsh. That was particularly evident within the neighbourhood I was speaking in.

It was tremendous to be able to share some words from the Bible and for the message to be listened to.

Before the evening ended, someone who had regularly criticized me came to offer an olive branch. It was in keeping with the evening's wonderful spirit of unity, humour and camaraderie. As everyone was leaving, a man said, 'Next time we should all invite our wives.' In a male-dominated community, such a statement was rare. It really had been a special night.

* * *

Three years after making her first visit to Albania, Joanne became the third member of our team in 1999. A chain of events culminated in this life-changing decision; the first link was her reputation as a top-notch baby-sitter. Regulars on her list were Calvin Young and his wife Pauline. Calvin was the assistant pastor of the church she attended. Joanne was a qualified nurse in her mid-twenties and worked on the children's ward of her local hospital. Calvin was a friend of Gary Spicer and had once joined him on a visit to Albania.

One night, whilst Joanne was on babysitting duties, Calvin suggested to her that she joined a group of people making a visit to Borsh.

'No!' she said without hesitation. It just wasn't the sort of thing she did. Joanne was shy and she lacked self-confidence. That said, she was greatly respected by her colleagues at work and looked after her father and younger brother at home, following the tragic death of her mother. She also played the keyboard in the church's worship group.

After going away to think about it, she changed her mind, and so she was a member of one of the first teams to visit me. One day, during her two-week visit, she had accompanied me to visit the wild-looking Razip. It was a hot summer's afternoon and Razip's wife thoughtfully provided us with damp towels to refresh our sticky fore-heads. A heavy weight had fallen on one of his feet as he worked on a building project in the village. Joanne cleaned and dressed his injured foot. Later Razip remarked, 'I saw the love of Jesus in Joanne.'

As Joanne negotiated the various stages of preparation for her long-term stay in Albania, I had no doubt about the course she was embarking upon. However, she had to work hard at patiently convincing others who had misgivings. How would she fare living in an environment that could be hostile and unforgiving?

During her final preparatory visit, made on the eve of the Kosovan refugee crisis, Joanne had decided that she wanted to lodge at Lida and Kimeti's home. They lived further up the rocky road from the base house. Their single-storey whitewashed home stood behind a white garden wall with an ornate blue metal gate. The couple shared a house with their teenage sons, Toni and Rakip. Kimeti had undergone an operation to remove a brain tumour two years earlier in Greece. Although the surgery had been successful, he had been left with partial facial paralysis; as a result his speech was a little slurred.

He often sat outside at a plastic garden table. On it there was a motor car wing mirror. He would pick up the mirror to examine his face many times throughout the day. As if to will his face back to normality, he would pull the skin just above his right cheekbone in order to stretch the flesh that sagged. Lida was a tall, attractive woman with dark, shoulder-length hair. She worked as a cleaner in what was once a well-used maternity hospital in the village. A downstairs room in the decaying building was used by the local doctor for consultations.

Whilst Lida was at work and his two sons were at school, time would drag for Kimeti. Because his mobility wasn't good, he remained housebound. To help fill the vacuum I visited him two mornings a week. I rarely came home without a bag of seasonal fruit from the trees in their garden. Although I felt it was right to go, I didn't always know what to do or say when I got there. Sometimes Kimeti would turn the television on and methodically flick through the channels until he found an English-speaking one for me to watch, such as *Euro News*. Television reception wasn't good.

One night, as our friendship matured, he invited me to watch international football. Albania was playing England in Tirana. The quality of the picture was so poor that at the end of the evening, having watched the full ninety minutes, I went home not knowing the final score! It was during those morning visits, when the house was quiet, that our relationship was forged. Kimeti didn't object when occasionally I prepared for my English lessons. Sometimes I practised my Albanian pronunciations with him. Other times he enjoyed talking about Albanian politics or recalling his days as a professional driver for the State. He appeared to have driven along every road in Albania; he was a mine of information about towns whose names I had seen only on a map.

Kimeti was willing for me to pray for him. Although he had recovered well from his tumour, he wasn't in the best physical shape. I would like to say that my prayers for a full restoration of health were immediately answered, but they were not. This was something I wrestled with at times. Was there an elusive formula I hadn't yet discovered? Eventually I came to accept that it's our duty to diligently pray for the sick. Beyond that, it's in the hands of our Creator.

After agreeing upon a figure of $75 a month for Joanne's room, Kimeti changed his mind the day before she was due to move in. He asked for considerably more money. At that late stage I didn't want to look elsewhere since so much about her new home seemed suitable. Reluctantly I renegotiated, eventually settling on much less than had been requested, but more than we had originally agreed upon.

As hosts, Lida and Kimeti provided safe and secure accommodation; just as Kristin's hosts, Muqo and Tonja did for Kristin. This was essential. Kristin told us that sometimes Muqo insisted on giving a prayer of thanks for the food before eating their evening meal, something that pleased her immensely.

With Joanne's arrival came an upgrade in communications. She had a portable computer with e-mail facilities and a mobile phone. As the village had no telephone land-lines, even the hit and miss success of Joanne's equipment was a huge improvement on what we'd had before.

Joanne became a faithful friend and colleague to both Kristin and me. Little by little she won the trust and respect of the Borsh people, eventually going on to open a health clinic in the village centre. She went about life quietly and efficiently, winning the hearts of many young mothers by giving pre- and post-natal care – usually in their homes. As our Land Rover became less reliable, it became necessary for us to travel by foot, sometimes walking six or seven hours in order to reach people living in distant hamlets. Joanne never baulked at the prospect of hard work, transferring the disciplines of nursing life in England to Albania, where medical care was relatively primitive. Carving out her nursing prac-tice took several laborious years. There have been occasional tears of frustration, even heartache along the way, but she stuck resolutely to the task. Few could have foreseen that such a shy and retiring person could go on to personify the objectives of our mission.

A pivotal figure during this time was a doctor called Norman How, from Long Buckby, Northampton. I had first met him during the cold, damp winter of 1997. He was doing a voluntary stint of duty at St Luke's Children's Hospital in Saranda. Regrettably, the English-funded centre had a short life-span. Norman had responded to an appeal for doctors made by the charity, 'Children in Distress'. I had been told that there were some English people temporarily living and working at the hospital, so I caught a bus into town one day to go and say, 'Hello.'

I liked Norman immediately. He had the friendly manner of an old-fashioned family doctor. Hovering around retirement age, he had a sharp mind beneath a loveable veneer of absentmindedness. A few days later, Norman went to the trouble of coming to Borsh for a few hours. He brought with him the hospital administrator, Stewart Shaller. Whilst walking together, we encountered several locals with medical needs. In every case he explained, in lay terms, the names and causes of the conditions. Back at the house, after a welcome cup of tea, the three of us prayed together.

'Please keep in touch,' Norman said.

Later on, I looked at the piece of paper he had left on the top of my bureau. After examining it for a few moments I was able to decipher his writing: 'God bless you Richard – you are in my prayers.' Below was written his home address and telephone number in England.

I enjoyed receiving Norman's letters. His faith, sensitivity and humility convinced me that the people of Borsh would benefit greatly if he agreed to make a further visit. Ten months after Joanne's arrival, he travelled from England to stay with me for a couple of weeks. Like all our visitors, he paid his own travelling expenses. At that time the people living in Ferme were encountering awful problems with their sewers. 'Black Water', as they call it, was backing up into their homes, which, as you can imagine, was particularly grim for them.

I had been asked to help out and had attended a meeting with the neighbourhood leaders to discuss the situation. Shortly after Norman's arrival, I told him about the problem.

His response was, 'I'll do anything you want me to; if that means digging up the roads, all well and good.'

Just for the record, I didn't hand him a pickaxe. Instead, he worked tirelessly in making medically-based home visits throughout Borsh; his attitude put those we visited quickly at ease. He patiently sipped *raki* – 'negotiating fluid' he called it, and ate food he wasn't used to.

Everyone made him welcome, accepting him as a friend. One day we visited Vasilika's mountainside home in Çoraj, situated in a distant corner of our patch. She had previously described to Joanne a gynaecological problem she was suffering with, but didn't trust Albanian doctors enough to consult them. One day she agreed to make the five-hour round trip, with Joanne by her side, to see a gynaecologist in Saranda.

Whilst waiting outside his room, her nerves got the better of her and she ran outside, refusing to go back in. On the day we visited with Norman, she whispered to me, 'I have no meat to give the doctor.' With great reluctance she accepted that it wasn't important to us. She went on to serve bread, tomatoes, olives and sardines from a big square table that she pulled into the middle of the lounge. Norman was able to examine her, and found that she had a fibroid problem. An accurate diagnosis to medical problems was highly valued. Kimeti for example, was told for nearly twenty years that his brain tumour was nothing more serious than a headache.

Norman's expertise considerably enhanced Joanne's local credibility. Working in partnership, the people's confidence in him was extended to Joanne too. However, she took care to repeatedly point out that her level of medical training wasn't as comprehensive as the doctor's. One morning Norman got up just after 5.30 a.m. to continue compiling a set of case notes for every person he had examined. This was something Joanne would use as a foundation for her own system of record-keeping.

Norman wasn't always good at finding a pair of matching socks in the mornings, but otherwise appeared to be a multi-gifted individual. When he wasn't wearing his doctor's hat, he regularly reached for his sketchpad and paints. Idle moments were taken advantage of: for example, when we had a flat tyre, he made a fine pencil sketch of the decrepit building the tyre repairer worked in. On a different day, he threw himself into helping me with an English class. The lesson was held in a grocery shop in the centre of the village. The shopkeeper, Roni, was keen for his two youngsters to learn English. He gladly made his premises available, arranging a small block of tables and chairs in the centre of his shop. Sometimes his daughter, Romina, had to interrupt her studies to serve a customer with a loaf of bread or a packet of washing powder. Whenever possible, I incorporated such moments into the lessons, teaching them the English words for whatever had just been sold. When Norman came they learnt some English medical expressions.

During his stay with us, Norman spoke of experiencing a spiritual deepening. He particularly enjoyed participating in the prayer times Kristin, Joanne and I shared together each morning. One day after prayers, as we sat together on the balcony, he told me an old Celtic word 'Anamcharja'. It means a coming together of souls, something he felt he was experiencing. As his stay drew to a close, he commented on Joanne's bright face coming into the house each morning.

'You're never miserable,' he told her with a smile.

On returning to England, he continued to act as a medical consultant for Joanne, by telephone, e-mail or letter. At times, his support was crucial.

* * *

Ann Landers is quoted in Kevin Gerald's book *The Proving Ground* as saying: 'Opportunities are usually disguised as hard work, so most people don't recognize them.'[1] My experience has been that good things have either happened during, or have come out of, times when I felt particularly pushed or tired. My meeting with a man on a boat crossing between Saranda and Corfu is one such instance. It would have been easier to have looked away after the initial eye contact, but instead we entered into conversation.

Englishman Chris Blake was once a Rolls Royce salesman in Hong Kong.

He told me, 'When people buy such an expensive car they expect everything to be perfect of course. You wouldn't believe how difficult it is to eradicate the irritating squeaks that cars sometimes make.'

He had since become involved in supplying aid to Albania.

'A difficult hole to get out of,' he said, with a hint of resignation.

As we went up on to the deck to get some fresh air, he listened with interest as I told him about the work of our mission. Little did I realize that this 'chance' meeting was nothing less than providential. He gave me the name and contact details of an Albanian man called Paulin, based in Tirana. As the leader of The Albanian Christian Centre, he sent out young believers as home missionaries. I put the piece of paper in a safe place: this would be followed up when time allowed. I had a deep-rooted desire to see a Christian church in Borsh, her leadership hewn out of Albanian rock. In meeting Chris Blake, I'd stumbled past a significant milestone on a long road that began with an idea, but ended in reality.

In order to understand better what the church in Albania has had to endure, one needs to know a little about the history of the country. I do not pretend to fully understand the legacy, so sacrificially made, by people whose faces I've never seen. In many, many cases their experiences have not been recorded by human hand. At times, religious history and political history are inseparable.

Using the first century as our starting point, there is New Testament evidence to suggest that Paul introduced Christianity to Albania. Some of those well-versed in Bible history reason that the geography of his missionary journeys would inevitably have taken him on to Albanian soil. In Romans 15:19 Paul speaks of preaching, 'All the way around to Illyricum.' This province included what we now call Albania. In AD 58 the Catholic historian, Farlati, wrote that there were seventy Christian families living in the town of Durres. In that first century, the illegal sign of the name of Jesus Christ was formed from crossing seven lines and one arch. Reported sightings of the symbols in ancient Illyrian basilicas, testify to the territory having been a breeding ground for Christianity.

In the fourth century, Roman Emperor Constantine declared Christianity an official religion. However, it wasn't until the fifth and sixth centuries that a comprehensive conversion to Christianity took place. The Illyrian church was directly subordinate to Rome until the eighth century.

Moving forward several hundred years to the fifteenth century, we come across Albania's national hero,

George Kastriot Skanderbeg. He galvanized his fellow countrymen into forcibly resisting the invading Ottoman Turks. Albanian history records that Skanderbeg and the Pope established close relations with each other, with a view to defending the church. Skanderbeg's stronghold was in the town of Kruje, from where he directed operations so successfully that the invaders were repelled for a quarter of a century. After his death in 1468 the invasion progressed, culminating in a complete occupation by 1501. The Ottomans ushered in Islam, which caused heavy damage to the Catholic and Orthodox Church. There were compelling reasons for turning to Islam: lower taxes in addition to better prospects of promotion in the civil service and army. By 1700, two-thirds of the population was Muslim.

During the nineteenth century the Ottoman Empire weakened and in 1912, in the coastal town of Vlore, Albania claimed independence. Fourteen years later, Ahmed Zogu, a former prime minister, proclaimed himself king of Albania.

On Good Friday 1939, Mussolini, the Italian fascist dictator, invaded Albania. The conquest was considerably eased by virtue of the fact that at the time, Italian advisors controlled Albania's army. Mussolini declared Albania to be a province of Italy.

As the Second World War progressed, Germany replaced Italy as invaders. Then, as Germany's occupation drew to a close, civil war broke out. Three sides battled it out; the Royalists, who wanted King Zog installed, the National Front and Enver Hoxha's Communist Party. Britain supplied arms to help Enver Hoxha fight the Germans. However, much of the military hardware was used against the other Albanian parties. In November 1944, the last German forces withdrew and Enver Hoxha seized control of the country.

He remained in power until his death from leukaemia in 1985.

In 1949, Britain and America despatched a contingent of trained expatriate Albanians, to plot the undermining of Hoxha, thereby destabilizing the entire Soviet bloc in the process. Many of them were shot before their parachutes had landed; the others were arrested and executed. The man responsible for co-ordinating communications between Britain and America was a spy, Kim Philby. He had informed Hoxha of what was coming.

During those days, a man from Borsh became famous. In 1940, Dervish Duma, after studying at the London School of Economics and settling in England, launched BBC Radio's Albanian Service. He went on to become a voice of hope for his oppressed compatriots back home. When Albania's borders were sealed, the Albanians living in England, now unable to get back to their homeland, looked to him as their unofficial leader. When the deposed King Zog fled to London with his family in 1941, Dervish Duma took him under his wing. The former monarch's landing in England had been a soft one: he and his family took up residence at the Ritz Hotel.

Immediately upon seizing power, the communist regime set about repressing both Christian and Muslim organizations. A large number of religious leaders were interned, imprisoned or executed. Enver Hoxha claimed that his eventual abolition of religion was for the good of the people. He declared that the Muslims had collaborated with the Turkish invaders; Orthodoxy was a pawn of the Greek government and the Roman Catholics had welcomed the Italian invaders.

In 1967, the State destroyed 2,169 'cult' buildings, including churches and mosques. The Youth Atheist Movement was the vehicle predominantly used to eradicate religious life. Many churches were turned into public halls; some were used for sheltering livestock, and others were completely demolished. Two hundred and seventeen clerics were imprisoned on false charges of exercising terror; many of them died in political prisons or were shot. The Catholic Church came in for particular punishment. It was described as 'a lair of foreign agents in Albania'.

In a book called *Scientific Atheism*, the ethos of those dark days was boasted about by some of Albania's approved authors. This is an excerpt: 'The ideological war against God today in Albania is aiming to liberate people from religious bondage. This is our dream. Down with God. Long live Communism! Atheism is our reason for living. What Hitler, Stalin, Mao-Tse-Tung and all other dictators failed to achieve has been accomplished by Enver Hoxha. We have closed down all churches and mosques.'[2]

In 1976 the Albanian People's Assembly adopted a new constitution. It contained specific legislation concerning the treatment of those citizens caught in possession of religious material. It was put into the same category as material considered likely to incite damaging propaganda and agitation. Should the confiscated items be considered a threat to State security, punishment was by 'deprivation of liberty' for between three and ten years. If the offence was committed in a time of war, or caused particularly serious consequences, the punishment ranged from ten years imprisonment to death. Article 37 stated that, 'The State recognizes no religion and . . . carries out atheist propaganda in order to implant a scientific materialistic world outlook.' The bleak wording continued, 'the creation of organizations of a . . . religious nature . . . religious activities and propaganda are prohibited.' Article 55.

Christians from the outside world worked to breach the high walls of atheism. The Christian gospel was broadcast into Albania: a few entered undercover to evangelize, others floated literature down the River Vjosa. That particular initiative was thwarted, when the authorities placed nets across the river.

Being aware of specific names may bring us marginally closer to the harrowing experiences of people martyred for their faith during those dark days. I consider myself to be all the poorer for not knowing the stories of countless others who died. In 1979, a man called Ernest Çoba died in a labour camp from police beatings. His crime had been to hold an Easter celebration in Shkoder. The following year Ndoc Luli baptized twins in his own family. He was sentenced to die slowly.

After Hoxha's death in 1985, Ramiz Alia came to power. There was no immediate easing of the anti-religious policy. In March 1986, the writer Hulusi Hako wrote in the Communist Party's publication, *The Way of the Party*, that, 'Religion and backward customs still have roots that have not been decisively destroyed. Religion was interwoven with the happenings, customs and thoughts of Albanian society, and injected its poisons in the joys and sorrows of life, from birth all the way to death.' In warning parents and teachers against religious influence, he called for a militant, atheistic education. In the summer of 1991 the communist regime finally ended. The people of Albania were free.

* * *

One warm May evening in Tirana I eventually followed up Chris Blake's recommendation to meet with Paulin Vilajeti. Although he had failed to arrive for our original meeting, I was not perturbed. Experience had taught me to treat missed appointments as routine.

'You English are good at time-keeping, unlike us Albanians,' I had been told countless times.

We eventually met later that day, by chance. As we drove towards each other on a busy city centre road, Paulin spotted my white Land Rover, with its Saranda plates. We stopped to speak, established our identities, and pulled over before the other drivers wore their horns out.

'Sorry I missed you earlier,' he said, as we shook hands.

In his mid-thirties, Paulin was stockily built and had a closely cropped, well-manicured beard. There was a compelling richness in his voice and his face radiated warmth. He had a lightness of spirit about him, a trait I had seen little evidence of in other Albanians. We went to the Café Europa to talk. The venue, I was told, was one of the first cafés to open in Tirana after the communists fell. Over a cappuccino he told me about something that had happened to him whilst his country was still living under the long dark shadow of communism.

It was 1988 when he came into contact with a westerner called Mike Diggens. The foreigner was officially a tourist, but as he wandered around the northern town of Pukë, he talked to Paulin about his Christian faith, something that was strictly prohibited by the authorities. When the tour party moved on, the ever-watchful security forces immediately took Paulin to task. 'What business did you have talking with a foreigner? What did you talk about?' He was incarcerated for three days up to his knees in water and beaten with a belt. Paulin confessed to nothing. The encounter was of considerable importance in his conversion to Christianity.

The following day we met again, this time at The Albanian Christian Centre. The grand old building had formerly been the Vietnamese Embassy. I met Paulin's blonde wife, Luli. Attractive and exuberant, she struck me as being quite westernized. Luli appeared to help Paulin keep the staff of the well-run centre on their toes. As Paulin and I talked together in his office on the first floor, I realized that in front of me was a man of great charisma and self-confidence. He told me about the day when electricity came to every Albanian home.

On 25 October 1970, the 'Festival of Lights' was celebrated. A unified national power grid gave electricity to every town and village. At that time he was a schoolboy, so he joined his classmates standing around his teacher, who held an electric light bulb in the palm of one of his hands.

'We just couldn't believe at first that out of it light would be given off,' he said.

'We all stared at it, thinking it was incredible. Gradually we became accustomed to having electricity and in time came to take it for granted. The novelty wore off.'

He then went on to make his point: 'When my country first opened up, the people couldn't get enough information about the Christian faith. They would eagerly take any amount of Bibles and Christian literature supplied by the foreign missionaries. People practically fought each other for whatever was being distributed. Then, as with the light bulbs, everyone got used to the idea of having religious freedom and began to ignore it. My dream is that one day people will be as hungry for the Christian faith as they were in those first days of freedom.'

We got on well together and parted as friends. In the following months Paulin, as well as other members of his staff from The Christian Centre, came to Borsh to meet some of the people and to get the feel of our mission's heartbeat.

Amongst those who visited were Paulin's brother-in-law, Bujar – not to be confused with my friend from Shkalle, and his wife, Xhina. I felt more at home with Bujar than with any other Albanian I had ever met. Now in his early thirties, he delighted in recalling his teenage years, when the State allowed the screening of European football matches. English teams featured regularly. When I told him that my drive to work back in England would take me near to the home of Aston Villa Football Club, he said, 'Ah, yes, Peter Withe and Gary Shaw.'

Inexplicably, he knew nothing about Wolverhampton Wanderers, but I didn't allow that to come between us. Bujar was a driver and maintenance worker at Paulin's Christian Centre. Xhina, elegant and pretty, with dark curly hair, spoke good English and worked as the Centre's administrator. Their stay at the base house was a happy one. Not only did we click together as friends – the way in which they related to the villagers gave me a glimpse of what the future could hold. How wonderful it would be to have the full-time presence of indigenous Christians working in Borsh. As a symbolic gesture of our intent to serve the Albanians, some of the English guests I was hosting washed Bujar and Xhina's feet. Upon their return to Tirana, they implored Paulin to commission some of the young graduates from his Bible training school to go and work in Borsh.

With the exciting prospect of Albanian co-workers becoming a possibility, there were also to be some trying days during that period. A local man accused me of excavating hidden treasure from his land, under the cover of darkness. He claimed that I had used what I had stolen from him to fund the repairs to the road. (Local men were continuing the work started by the refugees.) He tried calling my bluff, in an attempt to get money out of me, publicly declaring that he had a statement signed by witnesses that would incriminate me.

'Some people here are trying to break you,' a friend warned.

His absurd accusation was derailed after I voluntarily called at Saranda police station to put the matter straight.

Better news was waiting just around the corner. On my next visit to Tirana, I again met up with Paulin. Whenever I set foot inside the confines of The Christian Centre, I entered an oasis of relative tranquillity. In contrast to the grey, muddy streets outside, the colour and orderliness of the walled garden provided welcome relief. It was music to my ears when Paulin said, 'I'm going to send a newly wed Albanian couple to Borsh; they will work with you. It will be their job to become church leaders, building on the foundations you have laid.' Even though that wouldn't be for at least another eighteen months, I went to bed a happy man that night.

[1] Kevin Gerald, *The Proving Ground* (Tacoma: Kevin Gerald Communications, 1996).

[2] As quoted in the booklet *Determin'd to Save* (Albanian Evangelical Mission).

7

LOVE IS IN THE AIR

I hadn't enjoyed my school days, so a return visit to my secondary school, Ellowes Hall, was something I had mixed feelings about. I had been invited to drop in whenever I was next back in England. That moment came one autumnal morning. I wanted to thank the pupils for the several hundred pounds they had raised for our mission at a time when we particularly needed it. As I drove through the school gates, I was curious to see how the place had changed. Would any of my teachers still be there? Many of my memories were somewhat ignominious; would I see the old place through a different perspective?

As requested, I led morning assembly. I'd remembered the last time I had appeared on that stage, almost thirty years earlier. It was my tutor group's turn to lead morning assembly and we were going to sing a new song, 'Kum ba yah'. I was to join Bod, who remains a close friend to this day, in accompanying the group on our guitars. Whilst perched uncomfortably on high wooden stools, we twanged our way through the introduction. To our horror, the rest of the group missed their cue. One of us continued to play the song, whilst the other replayed the introduction. The result was not harmonious.

'Try again,' our teacher instructed from the sidelines.

116

Three times the song failed to take off, much to the glee of those watching. I'd sensed my ears were going pink and the more I thought about it, the more embarrassed I became. By now, even our teacher had her head down, her shoulders shaking. There wasn't a dry eye in the house.

Nowadays, assemblies are an all-standing affair. With over a thousand pupils in the school, they have to be conducted in two shifts. Before going on to tell them about my life in Albania, I talked about the one thing we all had in common: our schooldays. Certain areas of life that seemed deadly serious to me at the time, such as love interests, I could now look back on and smile about. When I was 14, I liked a girl called Diane. After several weeks of well-contained admiration, I plucked up the courage to telephone her. Two wrong numbers later, I asked her about going out to the cinema with me. She told me that it wasn't possible because she had to wash her hair. Although I didn't understand why that would take up a whole evening, I meekly accepted her rejection. I remained in a romantic wilderness.

Five years earlier, at junior school, I'd taken a playground fancy to Carol Jukes and decided I wanted to send her a Valentine's card. My brother Vin didn't want to be left out and became very upset. To stop his tearful protest, Mom ruled that his name, too, should appear on the card. Needless to say, our combined effort failed to turn the key to her heart.

After the assemblies, I enjoyed answering the questions posed by the several classes I spent time with. I particularly enjoyed being taken out for lunch by Mr Houston, my former PE teacher. At first it felt strange to be treated as an equal by him. As we devoured steak and kidney pie and chips, we chatted about his life outside school. Many years before, living under a cloud of insecurity, I would never have imagined that such an intimate exchange with a teacher was possible. One specific incident remains as keen in my memory as if it had happened yesterday.

The woodwork teacher used to gather the boys around his bench to give a practical demonstration. He would regularly tell rather risqué jokes. One day, when he was cutting out a dovetail joint, he looked up and his eyes fell on me.

'I'd better be careful what I'm saying,' he teased, 'the vicar's son is here.'

I laughed with all the others, but felt ridiculed and ostracized. Occasionally I was 'duffed up', a consequence of being the vicar's kid. This weighed very heavily on me at a time when being accepted counted for so much. Today, I drove out of the school gates, weaving between the hoards of youngsters, feeling sure of my identity and, at long last, able to laugh at myself.

Within a year, I was back at Ellowes Hall School. As a personal support fundraiser, close friend Jeremy Parkes organized a 'This is Your Life' event on my behalf. I received a much-needed cash injection, as well as many opportunities to laugh at myself. Former classmate Jimmy Watton told everyone about the time I mischievously gave him some laxative chewing gum. Mr Houston was another generous contributor.

'Why was I always in the second team at football?' I asked.

'Because we didn't have a third team,' he replied, with a sympathetic smile.

Visits to England could rarely be made without a shopping list of items to take back to Albania with me. On one occasion, Romi, the barber who cuts my hair in Saranda, asked me to get some good clippers on his behalf. I was given special privileges whenever I stepped into his chair. Not only would he quickly sweep away all the hair lying on the floor, he would also delve behind a curtain for a clean shawl to wrap around my shoulders. His attention to detail was, at first, something that surprised me. Never before have I had my nostril hairs clipped as part of a visit to the barbers.

I looked forward to my trips to Romi's because entertainment was practically guaranteed. One day I was in the chair when a policeman wandered in from outside. He rested his rifle against a wall and began preening himself in the large mirror facing me. Picking up the bottle of aftershave from the work surface, he splashed some on the back of his neck. When he was satisfied with his appearance, he picked up his gun and left. No words had been exchanged.

Romi took his time on deciding whether or not he wanted to keep the clippers. I'd gone to great lengths to purchase them from a specialist warehouse in England. Just before he finally decided that they were worth keeping, a rival barber stopped me in the street one day.

'I've heard you got some clippers for Romi; do you mind if I try them out too?' he asked. 'If I don't want them either, I'll be careful to pack them away again, so that the shopkeeper will never know they've been out of the box.'

Fortunately, Romi paid up, so I didn't have to suffer the embarrassment of requesting a refund next time I went to England.

As the last Borsh winter of the old millennium got wetter and wetter, our road repairs began to resemble sticky toffee pudding. Drier weather was needed for it to set into a firm, smooth surface. It didn't take long before people started complaining: 'You're ruining our road' and 'Every time I leave my yard, I get covered in mud.' Sihat was the works' supervisor and took the brunt of the abuse. The complainers didn't observe social niceties with him, unlike when they talked with me, a foreigner.

On a grey, wet morning I went to talk with him. He and the workers were waiting for the lorry to deliver its next load of raw materials. To add to the general misery of the situation, the lorry had broken down several times and spare parts were not readily available. As I approached, Sihat gave his usual cheerful greeting before he began to explain the work programme for the day to me. I stopped him and said, 'I've come to thank you for your hard work: I'm confident that your efforts will be appreciated by everyone that uses the road.'

For a moment Sihat looked astonished and didn't speak. Slowly a smile came to his lips and he held his right hand out to shake mine.

'Thank you very much,' he said, his face beaming in appreciation.

My words clearly meant a lot to him. What a difference a few words of encouragement make when uttered against a wind of prevailing criticism.

In Albania, the New Year celebration is the biggest holiday festival on the calendar. As the new millennium approached, it seemed as if the whole world was planning for a special party. For me, it was to be a low-key affair. Sihat had asked me to his place for supper and long before midnight I'd retired to bed. Early the next morning we met up for coffee.

'It looks as if it will rain yet again,' he said, disconsolately.

'I'd like to say a prayer,' I suggested.

He welcomed my idea and lowered his head. I prayed for his family in the coming year, for Albania's national leaders and for the road, that it would come good. During the previous evening he'd said that we should find wives for ourselves.

After my prayer he said, with a twinkle in his eye, 'Don't forget about the wives.'

It didn't rain after that for three weeks. The road dried out to form a hard surface and the moaners became our friends again. I grew to love a particular place where I could go to enjoy some of Albania's breathtaking beauty. Fifteen minutes walk from where I lived was a disused, forty-foot long concrete air-raid shelter. Only about eight feet wide, it had a flat, raised strip on top, which made a reasonably comfortable seat. Access to it was easy; it was just a few yards below the rocky road that links Borsh to the inland villages lying north.

It was a well-kept secret: few people visited and so I was able to enjoy it in peaceful solitude. Halfway up one side of the valley, the view of the mountain range opposite and the river below was stunning. Occasionally the sound of tinkling goat bells would be carried by the wind, along with the faint sound of distant shepherds calling to each other high above. It was a place where I regularly felt moved to pray.

From time to time I looked up to see a pair of eagles, effortlessly soaring on the air currents. Albania's national emblem is the distinctive image of a black, two-headed eagle against a red background. Nature majestically reminded me that I was indeed in the Land of the Eagles.

During winter months the place looked different. On chilly, clear days the sky was a beautiful crystal blue. When the weather closed in, clouds often hung just above the river, deep in the valley. Such moments at the long bunker made me mindful of a Bible verse taken from the book of James: 'What is your life? You are a mist that appears for a little while and then vanishes' (Jas. 4:14). Whenever I'm in danger of getting too big for my boots, those words put me back into place. I had bought a new wristwatch and had the words, 'You are a mist' inscribed on the back.

During the cold winter months I usually took a metal flask to the long bunker. I enjoyed a cup of coffee to warm me up. On wet days I took a plastic bag to sit on. Although I rarely saw other people, it became apparent that others saw me. Some people wrongly assumed that my flask was a metal detector and my visits were made in order to search for hidden gold. The story was widely circulated and didn't disappear. I was approached many times by men who wanted to go into partnership with me. Their proposals typically involved me purchasing and operating a metal detector and them providing the knowledge on where exactly we should look.

The 'gold-digger' story then became associated with my dramatic airlift a few years earlier. Some believed that I had found so much gold, I needed a helicopter to transport it all back to England. As time went on, I learnt to humour such suggestions. That was the case when an old village man insisted that I was a high-ranking British Intelligence Officer and Joanne was my private nurse.

Groundless insinuations never caused me loss of sleep, unlike the occasional rat that took up residency in my kitchen. At times, I would be woken by the sound of something moving about on the other side of the thin bedroom wall. When tell-tale signs appeared, I suspected that a rat, something I have a particular aversion to, was living inside the back of my cooker. By fortunate coincidence, my friend Bujar was visiting one night with younger brother Ilir, when the unwelcome guest appeared in the kitchen.

Sensing that I had no stomach for the chase, Bujar assured me that they would catch it for me. The terminology he actually used suggested that he somehow knew the rat was fatherless. The end came when the huge, brown rat was cornered and ran into a plastic bag lying on the floor. Ilir placed one foot on the open end of the bag and stamped with the other. At least it was a quick end. Ilir unceremoniously carried the bag to my front door to throw it outside into the darkness. The following morning Eqerem greeted me, looking a little shaken. He told me he'd found a dead rat sprawled across the top of one of his beehives. After that, rat poison featured on my shopping list, alongside bread and powdered milk.

* * *

Gary Spicer came to visit us a couple of times a year. Not only was he eager to review our mission's progress, he took an equally keen interest in how we were fairing individually. With Corfu so close, it was an ideal retreat; a place where we were free from constant scrutiny. I'm not a born motorcyclist, so shouldn't have been talked into hiring a scooter. Within half an hour I'd had two accidents, one of which caused a badly grazed right elbow, which I'd used as a brake as I slid along the road. When I took the damaged machine back to the hire shop, Gary was a tower of strength.

'I won't be able to come in with you, mate, I'd laugh too much,' were his consoling words.

Later, over a Häagen-Dazs ice cream – something that was much more my scene – he told me that he'd travelled to Zimbabwe in connection with setting up an orphanage.

'A man approached me there and said that God had prompted him to give the church a ninety foot gaff-rigged schooner he'd built. We're going to use it as a training vessel,' Gary told me.

I was delighted to hear that Theo Goutzios was to captain the boat named *Genevieve*. He had previously skippered the *Morning Star*, the boat I stayed on during my first visit to Albania. Theo and his wife Sandra were now based in Leptokoria in Eastern Greece where they ran a missions-orientated training base.

I had enjoyed spending some time with Theo when he visited Borsh eighteen months earlier with a group of South Koreans. I was interested to learn that South Korea is second only to the United States in sending out Christian missionaries from its shores. Just before his group of prospective missionaries departed, they stood and sang a blessing song to me. They wrote their names below the song's lyrics and laughed as I tried to pronounce their names. My Black Country accent must have sounded comical as I tried to get my tongue around, 'Hyun Suk Hong'.

In due course, I became an occasional facilitator of group devotional times on board *Genevieve*, when it visited nearby Greece. My sailing skills are akin to my skill as a motorcyclist. When it came to tying knots I was all fingers and thumbs. I couldn't understand why we had to go to the trouble of hauling sails up and down. We had a perfectly good engine that would have eliminated all that heaving and straining at the turn of a key.

This could not be said of a group of young firefighters, guests on *Genevieve* under the watchful eye of their leader, Neil McElvenny. He had tutored the youngsters, both technically, as a qualified fire-fighter, and spirit-ually, as an active member of King's Community Church. The trip was the culmination of their time under Neil's wing. His wife, Julie, who joined them, clearly had an affinity with the youngsters too. They loved life on board *Genevieve*, as much as they enjoyed their time in Borsh a few days later.

Always looking for a fresh challenge, the teenagers spurred each other on to conquer whatever lay ahead. That said, their exuberance never crossed the line into ill-discipline. One day, whilst in Albania, I drove the group to Blue Eye, a local beauty spot. A natural spring there forces its way up from below ground at a considerable pressure. The water is incredibly cold. Neil challenged two of the boys, Teddsy and Carl, to tread water for five minutes. If they could withstand the extreme temperature he would give them £50 each. Despite their screams, the two boys survived to claim their prizes.

I loved our devotional times, both on the sea and on dry land. I recall a particularly enjoyable discussion based on some words by Martin Luther King: 'One of the most agonizing problems within our human experience is that few, if any of us live to see our fondest hopes fulfilled. The hopes of our childhood and the promises of our mature years are unfinished symphonies.'[1]

Those words proved to be particularly poignant. Less than three years later, Teddsy's life was tragically cut short by a car accident, near to his home in Bedworth. He was 18 years old.

* * *

Sihat's New Year's Eve comment that we should find wives proved to be prophetic. A month before the firefighters visited, I'd driven him to meet a prospective wife. She lived in a village near the town of Patos, halfway between Fier and the oil-producing town of Ballsh. Sihat wanted my opinion and took my advice on buying some flowers, plastic being the only kind available, for Florika.

Once in her home, I barely saw her, because she remained in the background throughout. All the talking was done between Sihat and the male family members as we sat down to eat together. I hadn't been much use to Sihat on an earlier, unrelated mission. I had taken in everything I could about the girl who had appeared before me, only to be told that I'd got the wrong girl! Ultimately, my opinion was superfluous because Sihat and Florika wed the same year.

My own days as a single person were numbered too. Although I wasn't against the idea of remarrying, I was genuinely content with my single status. By the grace of God, I had found a richness in life that a few years earlier, pre-Albania, I couldn't have imagined. There were challenges of course, but the colour and intrigue of daily life more than compensated for the vacuum of emotional warmth.

Loneliness was something I had never experienced. The prospect of meeting someone, falling in love and wanting to marry, occasionally crossed my mind. However this wasn't without complications. What of my obscure lifestyle? It wasn't something I could prematurely walk away from. Additionally, I was a divorcee. Although remarriage would be acceptable in the eyes of the State, how would the church view it? If my personal circumstances were incompatible with church teaching, I would remain single.

On one occasion I requested a meeting with the leaders of my home church. Baring my soul before others, even though they were people I trusted, was less than comfortable. It was several months later when Gary, on a visit to Borsh, talked with me about how he and the other leaders saw things. He told me that, if in the future, I wished to remarry I could do so with the blessing of King's Community Church. Even though the way was open, life carried on much as before.

The first time I went to speak about our Albanian mission at Stockport Centre Church, I noticed Linda sitting in the congregation. Strikingly attractive, she was wearing white jeans and a blue jumper. She sat attentively as I gave my message. On my second visit, she came for supper at the church pastor's house. Pete Read and his wife Gill were good friends of hers. I drove her home at the end of the evening and asked if I could take her out for lunch sometime. We quickly relaxed in each other's company and it felt natural to be together. Unfortunately, we lived in two different worlds and a few snatched moments here and there were all that we could enjoy. We couldn't envisage those circumstances changing, so the proverbial line was drawn.

Three years passed by without seeing each other, then, during a visit to England, I thought how nice it would be to catch up with each other again. Occasional birthday cards and letters kept us loosely informed of what the other was doing. Linda's life had changed considerably. She had become involved with a missions organization, YWAM (Youth with a Mission), much to the surprise of her daughter Sophie and other family members.

When I tried calling her at the YWAM base in Nuneaton, a female American voice told me that Linda wasn't there: she had moved on. I tried her old home number and was delighted to hear her voice again. She said she would enjoy going out to dinner with me on the Saturday of that week. It would be good to hear how her life had been in the preceding years. If I'm honest, our forthcoming dinner date carried with it an element of romantic intrigue too.

Linda looked more beautiful than ever. It was a special evening, one in which I realized that my feelings for her, far from disappearing, were getting stronger. We had a lot to catch up on and our dinner date seemed to flash by. Albert Einstein once said, 'When you sit with a nice girl for two hours, it seems like two minutes. When you sit on a hot stove for two minutes it seems like two hours. That's relativity.' During the following days, I felt a growing sense of happiness when by Linda's side.

I returned to Albania a week later with a lot to think about. It wasn't long before I was making enquiries at Allways Travel in Corfu about a flight to Manchester, the nearest international airport to Linda's home. I was going to make a surprise visit, to propose to her.

With just a couple of days of the year remaining, I was sitting in the departure lounge at Corfu airport. The spectacular lightning from the storm lit up the sky every few seconds. It delayed the flight to Athens, which in turn meant that my flight to Manchester would be diverted to London.

Just before take off from London to Manchester, a woman boarded the plane late. With a baseball cap pulled over her eyes, and her head down, she was carrying a small child in her arms. I appeared to be the only person to recognize her: the other passengers carried on as normal without giving her a second glance. She sat on one of the seats in the empty row immediately behind me. It was Victoria Beckham. Together with her husband David, she invariably featured in the glossy magazines Joanne occasionally purchased from Corfu.

Like millions of others, I was interested in the photographs of her and her famous footballer husband. They appeared to live in a world full of fine clothes, cars and houses. I had idly wondered about their spiritual sustenance: they were worth much more than the beautiful things they possessed. I'd prayed for them, for a spiritual richness too. Maybe they had it already – if so, all well and good.

On that early Saturday evening, a day when Manchester United had been playing in London, I knew it was just a matter of time before Victoria was recognized by others.

I had discreetly handed her a piece of paper and said, 'Would you mind?'

She signed the back of my airport café receipt, 'Love, Victoria.'

After a few moments, I thought about my past prayer for her and her family. I realized that here was an opportunity to reach out to her in a simple way. I fumbled for another piece of paper and scribbled down some words from Proverbs 3: 'Trust in the LORD with all your heart and lean not on your own understanding; in all your ways acknowledge him, and he will make your paths straight' (verses 5–6). I added, 'May God bless you and your family.'

As I turned to address her through the gap between the seats I said, 'May I now give you something?'

After reading it, she thanked me. Her son Brooklyn kicked the back of my seat several times, something she scolded him for. Maybe he is to be a footballer like his father. Soon afterwards, the avalanche of attention started as her cover of anonymity was lost. After landing, we walked down the arrivals corridor together. I wanted to tell her all about Linda, that I'd secretly flown into the country to propose. I nearly fell into the trap of presuming to know Victoria, but in fact, all I knew was her famous face. I kept my secret.

After hiring a car, I headed for Stockport. As I drove, I imagined a variety of situations ahead of me at Linda's home. Maybe she would be out. What if she had friends with her? Would the special moment be thwarted somehow? I thought it would be a good idea to take a gentle sounding before knocking on her front door, so I pulled over at a public telephone. She was pleased to hear from me. Cars were streaming down the A6 as we exchanged greetings.

'Is that the sea I can hear?' she asked. 'Do you have electricity where you are at the moment?'

I told her that I wasn't near to the sea at present and that yes there was electricity. I didn't tell her it was the light inside the call box that I was referring to.

'If you could make a wish, what would it be for?' I asked her.

'I wish that I could see you now,' she replied.

'Yes, wouldn't that be nice?' I said.

After establishing that Linda was home alone, we bid each other goodnight and said that we looked forward to speaking again soon.

I jumped back into the car; two minutes later I was outside Linda's home. My heart was thumping with anticipation. I knocked on the frosted glass door and waited a few seconds. The door opened; Linda looked at me, gasped and quickly closed it again.

From the other side of the door I heard her say, with an expression part-horror, part-delight, 'Oh no, you've come all this way to see me and I haven't washed my hair!'

Was I to be struck by the hair-washing curse again? Fortunately the woman I wanted to marry didn't keep me standing on her step. When the door reopened, she said with a huge grin, 'I knew it was you, even before I opened the door. I recognized your knock.'

I had no doubts when I took Linda's hand and asked her to be my wife.

'Yes,' she said, 'I would love to marry you.'

Linda had completed two stints of mission work, in Kosovo and Turkey. There was a possibility of her volunteering her services to the Mercy Ships, a fleet that takes relief and medical aid to Third World countries. However, when I came along everything changed.

She loved me enough to say that she would join me in Albania, a great personal sacrifice. Her own life's path had led to an independent entry into mission work, so the 'two different worlds' situation no longer existed. Before we married, Linda came out to Borsh to take a look at where she would be living. The local people welcomed her with open arms.

Najda, Eqerem's daughter, said when she saw us together, 'You are the same.'

Her comment confirmed our own convictions of feeling that we were made for each other.

---

[1]   Coretta Scott King (Ed.), The Words of Martin Luther King (London: HarperCollins).

8

TEARS

Pathetic. A 44-year-old man snivelling his way through his wedding day. Even Linda, who didn't shed a tear all day, called me a big wet lettuce. I was hopelessly overcome with emotion and just couldn't get a grip. Since becoming engaged to Linda my tears button had developed an uncanny knack of turning itself on without warning.

One hundred and fifty guests joined us for the church service at King's Community Church. Linda had three bridesmaids: her daughter Sophie, and my 4-year-old twin nieces, Hannah and Rebekah. In the event, only Sophie and Hannah followed Linda down the aisle; Rebekah got cold feet. As the proceedings got under way, she overcame her nerves and came to sit on my lap. Gary Spicer and Pete Read conducted the service, and leaders from our mission partner churches prayed for us. Paulin was one of those who'd stepped forward to offer prayer. Together with his wife Luli, he had flown across from Tirana especially to attend our wedding.

It was a typical April day. Right on cue, rain hammered down just as we were about to go outside to have photographs taken. However, it would have taken a lot more than rain to dampen our spirits.

Paulin, saying a few words at our wedding breakfast warned in jest, 'Whatever you do, don't cry at your Albanian wedding celebration!'

By his side was Luli. In a black trouser suit and crisp white blouse, her warm brown eyes crinkled up as she joined everyone else in laughing at her husband's jibes. His comments were a reference to the wedding celebration Linda and I were to have back in the Albanian village where I had lived for the past six years. Paulin had noticed that I was going through the day wet-eyed, something an Albanian groom would never do. Back there, it is the bride's duty to cry, to show her sadness on leaving her family.

Looking back, my only regret on an otherwise glorious day is that when making my speech, I forgot to thank Vin for being my best man. This may appear to be a minor detail, but in recent years I had come to appreciate the value of true friendships more than ever before.

Twenty days later, we were back in Borsh preparing to pull our wedding clothes back on again. Not only did we want to share our joy with people I'd become attached to, we also wanted to celebrate our Lord's love for the people of Borsh. Surely this event, with a little thought, could complement the purpose of our mission.

Even though she'd be gazed upon by a sea of faces, all curious to see what an English bride looked like, Linda remained calm. In my case, however, the in-house butterflies made an early start with their manoeuvres. Questions flooded me as I lay awake in the early hours of the morning. Would the band turn up? What if we ran out of drinks? Would the invited guests come? Even worse, what if uninvited guests came? Early the next day, I went to see the proprietor of The Qasim Pali Café, our chosen wedding venue down in Ferme. Elez, our new landlord, had kindly donated several bottles of *raki*, but we needed to ensure other drinks would be available. On the way back I bumped into Edi's son. He played the accordion in the four-piece ensemble I'd booked for that afternoon. As he led the family cow to a place of pasture for the day, he reassured me, 'For sure we will be there.' They failed to show up of course.

The proceedings were planned to commence at 5 p.m. Earlier in the afternoon, Linda and I accompanied Joanne and Kristin to the Qasim Pali Café to prepare the room for the occasion. Joanne had made our Borsh wedding cake. Light snacks, plates of cakes and fruit were placed on the tables. Afterwards, several locals commented on how they thought light refreshments were preferable to huge plates of goat meat, the traditional wedding fare. Brightly coloured balloons were taped to the wall-mounted light fittings. I'd picked some pink wild flowers I'd noticed growing on adjacent wasteland. I thought they looked highly decorative in the white plastic cups I placed at intervals around the tables. In England the floral arrangements for both church and reception had been elaborate, a matter for careful planning, but here my impromptu effort did the job.

My next task was to shuttle some of our guests down to the venue. At the sight of several village friends dressed in their best clothes, faintly smelling of mothballs, my resident butterflies looped the loop. Most of the men wore white open-necked shirts under jackets. The women wore cotton floral printed dresses. Every few moments, my eyes returned to a narrow strip of road that climbs out of Borsh, hugging the mountain that rises steeply from the waters of the twinkling Ionian Sea as it winds towards the next village. It was from that direction that Paulin, who was to officiate at the event, would come.

With fifty minutes to go, there was no sign of him. As the passengers in our car commented on the high temperatures and joked that I did not have much time left to get changed into my wedding suit, I smiled. I was working out what course of action to take should Paulin not show. In England the bride's late arrival at the church is accepted as tradition. Our Albanian experience was that it was more the officiating pastor's prerogative to arrive late. With minutes to spare, Paulin arrived with teenage daughter Eva. In line with the village setting, they were both dressed casually.

Paulin drove us down to the café, where we were greeted with lots of handshakes and kisses. I felt proud of Linda who looked lovely in her wedding outfit, an ivory silk dress embroidered with pale pink rosebuds. In her hair, which she wore loose, was a filigree tiara of tiny pearl drops. She carried a single Aaron lily, a gift from the garden of one of our guests. Two seats had been placed for us in the centre of the room filled with about one hundred people. It was significant that the crowd represented each of the nine neighbourhoods that comprise Borsh. In past decades, the village was well known for three things: its huge orchards of citrus trees and olive groves, the prison on the sea front and its hard-headed inhabitants. There are exceptions, but generally there isn't a lot of goodwill between neighbourhoods. To see this rare coming together in an atmosphere that was warm and friendly gave us a great deal of personal pleasure.

I welcomed everyone and was relieved to get a response to my efforts at some humour. I was perspiring heavily under the grey wool suit, picked up in Corfu on my return to England to get married. My silk tie was purchased from Tirana especially for the event. During my time in Albania, I'd resolutely defended my bachlor-hood against the speculation that I must be miserable without a wife. From time to time village men would solemnly tell me that they wouldn't come to visit me for as long as I remained single. Who would serve them coffee? However, on this day, things had changed. I read words taken from Ecclesiastes 4:9, 'Two are better than one . . .' I was delighted to hear that, weeks later, Tonja, Kristin's landlady, was still repeating those words to her husband.

Another guest that day was Petrit, the local plumber. He was a stocky, ruddy-faced man with a well-receded hairline that exposed a bad scar. This had come from a bullet that had glanced his temple four years earlier during a dispute over how many drinks he had to pay for at the end of the evening. Many years before, he had offered to find me a loyal and beautiful Albanian wife if I paid him two hundred dollars. He sometimes wore a T-shirt with English writing on the front of it. The words, which he didn't understand, were a bad advertisement for his good-humoured offer. It read, 'If all else fails, lower your standards.' I should qualify this by telling you that I was absolutely sure this light-hearted banter had no root whatsoever in the sinister trade of human trafficking in certain parts of Albania.

After praying for us, Paulin spoke of why I had originally gone to live in Borsh. He talked about his own conversion and then moved on to tell the people of the hope they can have for the future through a genuine relationship with God. As he talked, everyone listened in silence. Small boys who curiously nosed their way into the crowded doorway were instantly silenced on making the slightest noise. Our guests were fascinated by Paulin's message. A living faith in God was being talked about with great passion by one of their compatriots.

After the formalities were concluded, everyone queued up to greet us and wish us well. Couples, families and individuals all demanded a photograph alongside us. Finally, we were given monetary gifts from each family, sealed in small airmail envelopes. For many this was a sacrificial gesture of love. In that moment I felt Albanian for the first time ever.

One of the invited guests who had his photograph taken with us was Pellumbi. Wiry-framed with a whiskery face, his tired eyes peered out from under his woolly hat. He was there without his wife Drita and their seven children. As established friends, they had all been invited, but just as Linda and I were celebrating a time of great happiness Pellumbi's family was entering a period of great difficulty. A day earlier, Joanne had met Pellumbi on the road and he had told her that their youngest daughter, 2½-year-old Zamira, had suffered a brain haemorrhage. She was in hospital in Saranda.

This family is both the happiest and the poorest one I have ever encountered. They live in a poor dwelling, a forty-five-minute walk away into the mountains. The family have a simple disposition and many villagers harshly condemn them as being not worth bothering with. As a toddler, Zamira, with her elf-like features and basin-cut hairstyle, always well wrapped up in numerous layers of second-hand clothes, would sometimes sit in the narrow road outside their humble home. She would pick up goat droppings and put them in her mouth. Her mother Drita, with her diminutive stature and cheerful disposition and ever open, smiling face, would look on benignly, without always stopping her. Advice on health education from Joanne and Kristin would always be eagerly listened to but was rarely acted upon. This over-relaxed, sometimes negligent attitude towards domestic hygiene was to bring ominous consequences.

The day after our wedding celebration Joanne caught the early bus to Saranda. The ninety-minute journey was made on the familiar boneshaker of a minibus. As ever, Joanne had been rocked to sleep by its motion long before Borsh's mountainous outline was out of sight. In Saranda better news than expected was waiting for her. The nursing staff at the hospital thought that Zamira's condition was in fact a bad case of anaemia. She had responded well to a blood transfusion and three days later she was back home. In an attempt to make her frail body stronger, Joanne ensured that Zamira received a regular supply of multi-vitamin syrup. Her general condition, however, deteriorated. Occasional visits to Saranda to receive blood transfusions gave only short-lived relief. We were distressed to be told that leukaemia had been diagnosed.

On a hot summer afternoon, ten weeks after her discharge from hospital, the gravity of her condition became clear. Joanne accompanied a group of visiting friends from England to the remote, beautiful neighbourhood where Zamira lived. On entering the house she saw Zamira's motionless body lying on a grubby bed. At first Joanne thought that she was looking at a corpse, but was relieved to find a pulse. She called the others in from outside. Zamira's brothers and sister crowded in with their visitors to offer words of prayer. In the dimly lit room, flies buzzed about as all heads were bowed in a moment of great sadness. Drita had been told that nothing more could be done for her daughter at the hospital in Saranda. She could hold back the tears no longer.

The following morning, Drita and Pellumbi, carrying Zamira in their arms, travelled to Tirana. Could help be found there? There was no news for a week and then on the eighth day Pellumbi returned alone. Things were not going well. It was the holiday season, so although they had been able to get Zamira admitted to a children's hospital, only a few staff were on duty, so no one was around to give her a thorough examination. Jo, Linda and I talked it through; at the least I should accompany Pellumbi back to Tirana, to give him moral support. Pellumbi was OK with the idea, so at 4 a.m. the following day I collected him from his home and we headed northwards.

My experience has been that most Albanian men are great talkers, especially when in the passenger seat of my car. Pellumbi wasn't. I didn't mind, I appreciated the thinking time. Questions started to form in my mind. What if, once in Tirana, I couldn't understand the medical terminology in the Albanian language? What if we were expected to cough up the customary financial gifts to the doctors in return for their services? Pellumbi was without lek at the best of times and the money I had in my pocket wouldn't stretch far.

After a brief coffee stop in Vlore, we recommenced our journey, breakfasting on a bag of bread and bananas. Some words came to me, elevating my thinking to a different plane, 'Do not be anxious about anything, but in everything, by prayer and petition, with thanksgiving, present your requests to God' (Phil. 4:6).

'We need to pray,' I told Pellumbi, feeling something of a clot that I hadn't mentioned it before.

As we approached Tirana, Pellumbi told me that he couldn't remember the location of the hospital Zamira had been admitted to. I likened the capital's traffic flow to a huge dodgem car ring. I caused the crescendo of horn-blowing to jump up another octave by stopping on the side of the road to ask for directions. Children's Hospital Number Three was located after forty noisy minutes.

As we made our way up the stairs we passed a plaque on the wall stating that the hospital was mainly funded by EU funds. Zamira was in a room with two beds, one wooden, one made of tubular steel. At the end of one of them was a small table. The water supply wasn't constant, so there were several bottles of water standing at the base of a washbasin. Just above Zamira's bed was an electrical socket, covered with a well-fingered piece of masking tape. Patients were expected to provide their own soap, towels, crockery and cutlery.

Zamira was sleeping soundly and only stirred when Drita tried to turn her over. When this happened she cried bitterly and tried to pull free the small tube, inserted into one of her arms. Her skin was yellow and although her fingernails were still caked in dirt, she generally looked cleaner than when she was at home. It was lunchtime, so Drita wandered off down the corridor to the food trolley. She returned a few minutes later, clutching a small plastic food container full of stew.

The paediatrician on duty, Dr Raida Petrela, was to play a crucial role in Zamira's fight for life. Communicating with her was easy because she spoke English.

'My work once took me to a hospital in Manchester,' she told me.

As we walked along the corridor to her office I heard the sound of her high heels clicking on the floor tiles. In her late thirties, her well-groomed hair and bright lipstick were signs of a woman who took pride in her appearance. I suspected that the heaviness under her eyes was a consequence of long working hours.

From the other side of her small desk she said, 'I will do all I can to help.'

She told me we would not have to pay for this. Her manner was serious throughout, but with good cause.

'It will be a miracle if Zamira survives,' she said candidly.

On a pad normally used for writing prescriptions she wrote the word 'Leshmaniosis'. I found out that

Zamira's illness is also known as Kalazar disease. A microbe was eating her spleen.

A month later, Zamira was discharged from hospital. She had been given the normal treatment for the disease. However, after two weeks back home it was clear that she was not yet out of the woods. Drita agreed that we should make another visit to Dr Raida. By now our vehicle had developed problems, so we decided to make the long journey by bus. In the event Drita didn't show up. To our dismay she had decided to go to a 'people's doctor' in another town. Her thinking had been that traditional methods had not helped. She had sought an alternative, but the potion of muddy water in the bottle she'd returned with looked anything but a likely remedy.

'She heals people depending on the position of the moon,' Drita said.

Eventually she agreed that Dr Raida's expertise was more likely to produce a positive result. Early the following morning Drita carried Zamira four miles to the place where the bus to Tirana would stop. She had no teddy bears or dolls to accompany her on the journey; only an orange flower that Drita had picked along the way.

Jaundiced and listless, Zamira gave me a sad stare that seemed to say, 'No more, I just want to die.'

Upon our eventual arrival at the stark concrete building that houses the children's hospital, a duty nurse told us that Zamira was in urgent need of a blood transfusion.

'Do you have any syringes with you?' she asked.

I shouldn't have been surprised by her question but found it remarkable that such essentials weren't readily to hand. Outside of the hospital's muddy grounds I located a store that sold the syringes and quickly returned to waiting nurse and patient.

As I left the hospital for the night, the nurse reassured me, 'Don't worry, everything's going to be all right.'

In the following seventy-two hours, I walked many miles through the city's dilapidated streets. In my pocket I was carrying samples of Zamira's blood. Dr Raida had given me directions to a private laboratory where a reliable analysis could be given. Cats, dogs and the occasional cow scavenged through the numerous piles of rubbish I passed on the way. Getting the results communicated back to Raida proved to be frustratingly difficult. Ultimately, she was able to establish that Zamira's body was rejecting the treatment.

Zamira had bravely endured three separate periods of hospitalization including the current one, but with the onset of winter came a further decline in her condition. There were whispers of it being a hopeless case, but these didn't come from Dr Raida's lips.

I often accompanied Pellumbi when he travelled from Borsh to visit his wife and sick daughter in Tirana. Our hearts went out to them as a family; they had other troubles to worry about as well. In their absence, a married man from nearby harassed their elder daughter, Eliona, who was looking after her five younger brothers. The village offered little sympathy. I overheard several people say, 'Well, if Zamira dies they'll just have another child.'

One particular visit to Tirana both started and finished miserably for Pellumbi. During the journey, the bus driver's mate, a Borsh man nicknamed 'Dracula', owing to his unusual dental work, loudly accused Pellumbi of stealing olives.

'Or are they God's olives?' he asked sarcastically.

In fact, Pellumbi had picked the olives at the owner's request in return for half their sale price. Pellumbi maintained a dignified silence throughout. On the return trip, he had a bag of children's clothes, purchased from a rag market, stolen from the bus' luggage hold.

On one occasion Raida, who had by now asked me to call her by her first name, asked me a question: could Zamira be taken to Italy or England for treatment instead? We were in a café close to the hospital entrance; many of the medical staff sat around, drinking coffee together and chatting in friendly huddles. It seemed that although Zamira's illness was within her field of expertise, Raida had reached an impasse. It was looking bleak again. Raida's idea wasn't practical: we simply didn't have enough time to negotiate the many layers of bureaucracy involved in securing foreign travel permits.

'I'd like you to continue treating Zamira here in Tirana, subject to my getting the medication sent in from overseas,' I said.

She gave her espresso coffee another stir and her eyes returned once more to mine. I sensed that such faith in her abilities was a rarity. My appreciation of her professional approach, observed during several visits to her ward, was in marked contrast to the way she was spoken to by the majority of parents.

'The families of many sick children often leave it too late before they come to us,' she said.

'When they eventually get here they often demand with menaces that I treat their children in a specific way, even though they have no medical training. Sometimes it's like dealing with terrorists.'

She smiled but her point was serious.

I'd heard incidents of Albanians being treated in neighbouring countries, but wouldn't it be wonderful to demonstrate to the outside world just how competent Albanian doctors could be? Raida seemed to be encouraged by this and we gradually uncovered a new way forward. Although Zamira had rejected the treatment, this didn't necessarily signify a wrong diagnosis. There was another drug in existence, but at £5,000 for an individual course of treatment, it was too expensive to most people. Furthermore, Raida had no experience of working with it.

What could be done? Who could we refer to? Our great friend and occasional visitor to Albania, retired GP Norman How sprang to mind. He was only a telephone call away, or to be more precise, a fax message away. Norman was always eager to help. With his extensive network of medical connections, a new range of possibilities could open up to us. As Raida returned to her ward I went to make some urgent phone calls from the call box in the hospital grounds.

At 4 a.m. the next morning there was neither electricity nor water. I fumbled about in the dark to get dressed and woke the night watchman to let me out of Paulin's centre where I'd been sleeping. The streets outside were wet, cold and empty. I needed to be up and about early in order to catch the only bus back to Borsh, which left before daylight. Raida had organized a bed for Pellumbi at the hospital about thirty minutes away, and after collecting him we made our way to the old football stadium to catch the bus home.

Drita stayed on with Zamira in the austere hospital room. Although little could be done medically, the nurses were kind and friendly towards both of them. Home conditions were even less comfortable, so I gave Drita some money to make their stay as pleasant as possible. A stall outside the hospital gates sold fruits and other food that wasn't available back in Kriz. There was also the novelty of a photographer who regularly visited the children's wards to take instant photographs of the youngsters. Drita proudly showed off her print to other mothers and hospital workers.

Frozen fields made for interesting viewing from the bus windows; my mind turned to Linda. How good it would be to see her again. I also thought about Zamira, imagining new wheels beginning to turn for her far beyond Albania's borders. I tried a chocolate bar I'd bought the night before, a 'Kat Kat Tat' bar. Albania's answer to the Kit Kat was a great disappointment. Several of the other passengers produced food from their bags. The metal ashtrays on the backs of the seats came in useful for cracking open their hard boiled eggs. Salami, olives, goat's cheese and bread all seemed to go down well.

As the journey progressed southwards, snow began to fall. The mountain peaks usually got a covering during winter months, but to see snow sticking at ground level was unusual. The bus driver announced that we couldn't make our way home by the normal route. A driver passing in the other direction had stopped to advise him that a road we intended to use was closed. The journey became a thirteen-hour epic. We were dropped off from the bus ninety minutes away from Borsh. Fortunately we got a lift with a man who was prepared to risk the treacherous roads.

As we approached Borsh, Berti, our driver, had to stop the car. All the vehicles in front of us were stationary. Despite the serious nature of events at the time, even Pellumbi laughed as he looked ahead. Grown men, lorry drivers included, had stopped for a snowball fight. Apparently it was the first time in seventeen years that heavy snow had fallen. One little lad was dancing with joy as the snowflakes fluttered down all around him. When a couple of icy snowballs thudded against Berti's car, he jumped out to threaten the offender. However, there was no fear of police involvement; they were busy making a snowman.

In the following days, telephone conversations with friends in England – often conducted from remote hillsides by mobile phone – confirmed that Dr How had indeed opened the doorway to the world-renowned Tropical Diseases Unit in London. Some of the best brains in the world were considering the faxed case notes of a gravely ill little girl from a desperately poor family in the mountains of southern Albania. Simultaneously, an appeal to raise the funds required to pay for the rare drugs, if their release was sanctioned, was launched by our church back in England.

Further twists in the story lay ahead. Despite the offer of unrestricted hospital accommodation for herself and Zamira in Tirana, Drita decided to return home with her daughter. Time was running out and the shadow of death was creeping closer. Everything possible to help her hold onto life had been done from within Albania. Joanne, who faithfully cared for her, began to fear that even if the drugs could be flown in from England, Zamira was so weak that yet another long and cold bus journey to Tirana could kill her.

Ten days before Christmas we received an early present. The release of the drugs was duly sanctioned and before the appeal fund gained momentum, the drug suppliers generously donated their product as a good will gesture. Drita and Pellumbi bravely agreed to a 'make or break' journey to Tirana with Zamira. Upon their arrival at the hospital, an abusive and drunken doorman gave them a verbal battering.

'You've wasted your time coming here. Your girl will die anyway.'

Fortunately, the greetings were more cordial up on the familiar children's ward.

A couple of days later, Yvonne, a lady from our church's missions office, stepped onto an aeroplane with the medication in her hand luggage. The healing process that so many people were praying for could finally begin.

* * *

On the day of our first wedding anniversary, Linda and I enjoyed calling in at our young friend's home deep in the mountains. Dimly lit, with flies still buzzing around, two children wrestled over a bag of sweets. Zamira, sitting on a bed, tugged at one end of the bag. The other end was firmly secured between her brother Tinker's teeth as he sat on the floor. In order to gain better leverage she rested both feet on his face and pulled for all she was worth. Their mother said, 'Zamira is very strong,' and smiled.

Zamira's survival was cause for celebration. Her story, more than any other experience in my life, taught me a salutary lesson in never giving up. At times her life had been hanging by a thread, with little hope of recovery. When she was at her lowest ebb, even Pellumbi spoke of 'gently letting her go'. We had little in our hands to work with; to most, her plight had been hopeless. Many Albanians think of Lord Byron, who once visited Albania, when they think of English poets. For me, some words of another Englishman, G.K. Chesterton, were particularly apt. He once wrote, 'Hope is the power of being cheerful in circumstances which we know to be desperate.'

9

GIVE ME THAT MOUNTAIN

Linda and I had set up home in what resembled a white doll's house, near to the centre of the village. Surrounded by vines, fig and orange trees, the tiny concrete house stood in the garden of the couple who'd built it: retired teachers Elez, and his wife Polikseni. Niti, their son who was in his thirties, also lived with them. Niti had been struck down with a muscle-wasting illness just as he was beginning to enjoy his teenage years.

Elez was a workaholic, constantly tending the vegetables in their long, sloping garden; harvesting their many olive trees or painting signs for the local seaside restaurateurs or people with rooms to let for the summer. Garden seats, steps and even the lower wall of our house were adorned with Elez's shell sculptures. Poli's demeanour was stern, but we quickly came to appreciate her kind-hearted friendship. She regularly brought dishes of hot food across within moments of our arrival home after a day's work. She was a good cook: we particularly enjoyed her *byrek*, a traditional pie made from potatoes and filo pastry. However, not all of her creations were for consumption, such as the plate of hot, mushy onions she rubbed into Linda after a fall down our metal staircase. It was, she said, a village remedy for bruising. Ironically, earlier that day Linda had prohibited the use of onions in my sandwich because they would make my breath smell.

Our rented house was little more than a one up, one down, but Linda's feminine touch transformed it from a house into a genuine home. Thanks to the efforts of some visiting friends from England, a sink and cold water supply was installed into the tiny kitchen. There were no doors or stairs inside, so food had to be taken upstairs via the staircase outside. On rainy days our chips got wet.

The animal kingdom played a big part in our domestic life, some animals staying longer than others. When rats moved into the roof, Elez responded, 'No problem, they come and they go.' A pretty tortoiseshell cat took a liking to Linda's cooking. It appeared to welcome a change from its regular diet of large grasshoppers, whose male population sang a shrill, chirpy song when, according to a book I had read, temperatures exceeded 23 °C. The cat gave birth to a kitten in the back of an old settee we had on loan from Poli. Early one summer's morning, I had to tackle a four-foot long poisonous snake I'd spotted resting at the foot of a wall near our kitchen. Using the only tool I had to hand, I clubbed it with a hammer. As it wriggled about on the ground, the cat eagerly devoured it.

I had a shock when visiting the bathroom one evening. We had a western toilet, as opposed to a traditional Turkish one, and upon flushing it something jumped out at me. It was the first time I'd ever experienced two-way traffic when making such a call. A frog narrowly missed my legs and came to rest on the washbasin. If we'd eaten toad-in-the-hole for tea I may have been less surprised. The following day it returned, taking up residency on our showerhead. Once again I moved it on, but it wasn't easily discouraged. Perhaps our bathroom had been, or was to become, a spawning ground.

From the onset of my involvement in the mission, I was keen to communicate the day-to-day detail of life to friends and supporters back home. I prepared a monthly report and financial summary in order to remain accountable to our sending church and its partners. Additionally, a monthly newsletter was produced to describe the people, places and situations that come across our path. As Linda and I were going through our frog era, I entitled the newsletter, 'Frog in the bog'. This edition drew more comment from our correspondents than any other. The frog, which encouraged many of its cousins to also visit, eventually moved on when it felt ready.

Less welcome were the droves of ungainly black scorpions that saw our home as a drop-in centre. They had been only occasional visitors to the base house, but here there was the distinct possibility that we were living near to a nest. It was impossible to anticipate when you would next be in their silent presence. Sometimes they would be found curled up inside an empty shoe. Another time one would suddenly appear halfway up a wall, when moments earlier there had been no visible evidence of it. Not only are they very ugly, but they also have a sting worse than that of a bee. The locals warn that the beige ones are deadly, so we counted ourselves fortunate that we only hosted the black variety. Linda and I employed different techniques for their removal. If I came home to see blobs of green blood splattered on a wall, I knew that Linda had been wielding her executioner's hammer. My approach was equally quick, but subtler: I squashed their heads with the end of a pencil.

To complete the menagerie, a living dustbin came in the form of our landlord's donkey. On the other side of the garden gate which, thanks to Elez's handiwork carried our names, stood its wicker stall. Technically, Elez owned only half of the donkey: the other 50 per cent belonged to a neighbour. In the absence of a corporate refuse collection system, the donkey gratefully munched its way through all our unwanted food, such as potato and orange peelings. We burnt combustibles and took the rest of our garbage, well-wrapped, into Saranda for dumping into one of the street bins there.

Some of our friends who came to stay also shared in our friendship with Elez's family. Peter Robson, an eminent neurologist, and his wife Mary stand out in particular. Peter made strenuous efforts to identify and cure Niti's rare condition, but sadly long-term relief proved elusive. However, his commitment to help will always be appreciated by Niti and the rest of his family. The same can be said of Jeff Burgoyne, from Living Hope Church in Dudley. After meeting Niti, he went home and raised the funds to buy a suitable vehicle that could transport the snacks Niti sold to children outside the school gates.

'You have given my son a new pair of legs,' Elez told Jeff when the gift was handed over.

The warmth with which the village people received Linda was not a flash in the pan. How good it was to have her by my side. I enjoyed the fact that we were sharing these experiences, times that we could look back on together. Her own integration was helped enormously when she began teaching the next wave of children who were interested in learning English. Although many families had previously told me that their door was open to me day and night, as a married man I became a more acceptable proposition. For example, my friendship with Eldion's family, the boy who had begun to learn English on a makeshift desk in his garden, matured further, thanks to Linda's presence. His sister, Ariana, now a qualified teacher, had herself been a keen English student and enjoyed conversing with Linda. Their mother, Sanxho, had once let me milk their cow. I squeezed and pulled at its udders until a sweat formed on my brow, but only managed about half a pint.

'She must be empty,' I protested.

Sanxho later came back with a bucketful.

Sanxho's father, Mahmut, was a likeable old man. He lived with Mine, his Romanian wife in a modest home on the seashore at Shkalle. A great lover of history, he relished telling stories to anyone who would listen. Not long after Linda and I married, we took our wedding pictures to show them.

'Stop telling your stories, I want to see the photographs!' shouted Mine.

Mahmut gave as good as he got. 'Be quiet, old woman,' he replied. 'Richard wants to hear my story.'

Sadly Mahmut developed a skin cancer on his face. I took him up to Tirana to try and get it treated and Dani, one of his sons, accompanied us. The outlook though was grim: the only laser in the country was broken, with little prospect of repair. Securing papers to get treatment in Greece was impossible. Mahmut died peacefully in his sleep one night, from unrelated causes. The funeral was held the following day, in keeping with Muslim tradition, at the small cemetery in Borsh.

Shako the carpenter made a simple coffin that was slatted underneath. Nazmi, Sanxho's husband, transported the body to the cemetery, along with the chief mourners, in his grocer's van. Afterwards, I was invited to attend the wake, and with fifteen other men, clambered on to the back of an open-topped truck. Hanging on for all I was worth, we made our way down a road lined with olive trees. The branches of the trees catapulted back at us as we bounced our way towards the family home.

At the house, the men and women were segregated. In the centre of the room allocated for the men was a table piled high with cigarettes, the customary gift for the family of the deceased. After thirty minutes or so, the men were invited upstairs to consume the food prepared by the women the night before. There was a dignity about the whole occasion that I'm sure Mahmut would have approved of. I can imagine him being disappointed when people started leaving. He would probably have said, 'Stay a bit longer, I haven't finished telling my stories yet.'

* * *

The greeting 'May you have a son,' was a greeting passed on to Linda and me almost every day. Sons were doted on, daughters less so. In the eyes of the villagers, our crowning glory would have been the arrival of a baby boy. As we had married in mid-life, we were unlikely to be blessed with children, much to the disappointment of the locals. With the exception of people like Poli, intrusive questions about the timing of our first birth came from practically every quarter.

One day, someone tried pinning me down for an answer to the question, 'Who has the defect, you or your wife?'

When I explained that Linda and I had married because we loved each other, I was given a quizzical look – what a strange notion. The collective view was that newly married women produced children. What other use could they possibly have?

Other eventualities came along that took our minds off every thing else apart from keeping life and limb together. One day, Linda and I made the return journey from Saranda with Landi, a minibus driver who competed for

passengers with minibus owner Altin, and long-estab-
lished coach driver, Ermir. Usually the biggest question
mark hung over how many passengers, baggage, animals, vegetables or minerals he would cram into the
vehicle built for a maximum of nine people. On the day
in question, Landi became increasingly erratic in his
driving. He took risks on blind bends high up on the
mountain roads, forcing him to swerve and brake hard to
avoid oncoming vehicles.

As we pulled into Borsh I asked what the problem had
been. He told us that he had some fresh fish in the back
and, as it was such a hot day, he was anxious about it
going off.

'Was Linda frightened?' he asked, with a grin.

'No, of course not,' I said, as we walked off down the
lane towards home. In time, our stomachs returned to
their usual places.

Paulin, a man of honour, fulfilled his promise to send
Albanian graduates from his Bible School. With their
arrival, I knew that my work as a pioneer should and
would draw to a close. Although we wouldn't move on
for another eighteen months, the last chapter of my full-
time Borsh residency had begun.

Shkelqim Nazeraj (nicknamed Çimi) and his fiancée,
Danja Vogli, were the couple Paulin had earmarked for
full-time service in Borsh. Çimi was born in the mid-
Albanian town of Ballsh, at the heart of a once efficient
oilfield. Nowadays, the heavy spillage from the ancient,
leaking drills all across the area has created an environ-
mentalist's nightmare. Danja came from the town of
Kruje, famous for its links with Skanderbeg, Albania's
national hero. Both in their early twenties, they were of
average Albanian height and build. Çimi was round-
faced and had straight, black hair. He was fluent in
Italian and had a reasonably good grasp of English.

Danja, a competent seamstress, whose hair was a little lighter, had a tendency to look melancholic, an expression that was transformed when she smiled. Originally from Muslim backgrounds, they were converted to Christianity before going on to join a church building team in Çimi's home town.

At times this landed them in hot water, but they came through it all the stronger in their faith. Before getting married in July 2001, they spent several weeks in Borsh, an insightful period of induction at the beginning of a five-year commitment. During those days we got to know each other a little better. It was clear that they too would have to work hard to win over the inhabitants of Borsh; their common nationality was no guarantee of acceptance. Çimi and Danja were accompanied by three associates from their base in Tirana for this preliminary visit. Danja devoted herself to cooking for the whole group throughout their stay in the base house.

One day Linda and I accompanied Limi and Juli, together with Lili their female team mate, on a visit to a man called Aslan. He was in the process of constructing a simple summer residence in Shkalle. As we were walking past, he called us in and asked if we'd sit and talk with him for a while. A retired metallurgist, he normally lived in Tirana, but enjoyed summertime by the sea.

It was a fascinating encounter. Aslan was old school: a hard-nosed atheist who had enjoyed the rare privilege of foreign travel during the former regime's time in power. Only the select few were allowed to see life outside Albania during those days. His professional seniority had opened that very narrow door for him. What was it like to travel abroad at that time? Albania's political dictators brainwashed the masses into believing they were the only nation in the world with enough bread to eat.

How did he react when he saw that far from starving, people in other countries were prospering beyond the imaginations of his compatriots? Did he grow to resent the State machine that churned out such deceitful propaganda whilst repressing his countrymen? Aslan, slightly built with pale blue eyes and thin grey hair swept neatly back, thought for a moment.

'I wasn't stupid,' he said, 'I knew it was in my own best interests to keep my mouth shut about what I had seen abroad, so I said nothing.'

Our young friends asked him about his belief in God. He responded by saying that he had a poor opinion of what he had seen and heard of priests from neighbouring countries. He didn't accept that a God existed.

Whilst respecting his views, our teenage friends, who were too young to have experienced the harshness of life under the excesses of Enver Hoxha, explained why they believed in God. They described what their Christian faith meant to them and why they had such a positive hope for the future. Their arguments, when expressed in the Albanian tongue, were refreshing to hear. The majority of the Borsh people appeared to view life through a doom and gloom perspective. This outlook had been fashioned by the severity of their past and a feeling of hopelessness towards the present. The new order was, they said, riddled with corruption. It would be untrue to say that Aslan changed from his position as a battle-hardened sceptic. What Linda and I had witnessed, however, was a meeting between two different generations. God willing, there would be many more such encounters.

I had made it my practice since my first days in Borsh to begin every morning with prayer. Now, with Çimi and Danja alongside, these prayer times became even more precious. Albanian tongues uttered their own petitions of prayer and adoration to God. That would have been unimaginable a few years earlier. Scripture readings were also shared: how wonderful to hear Çimi and Danja read from the book of Proverbs!

We were given the use of an abandoned flat in Ferme to use as a meeting place on Sunday mornings. Our gathering would, of course, have aroused a degree of curiosity to those looking on. A sign on a wall read, 'We have come to pray for the people of this village. If you would like to join us, please do so.' Dino and Lili, who lived upstairs, kept the key to the flat, which contained only a couple of worn out wooden-framed settees. Dino, a habitual card player, came down one morning to tell us about the large amount of money he'd gambled away the previous evening. He wasn't looking for a cash gift or even for divine guidance in his next game. He simply wanted to talk and welcomed a word of prayer for him and his family.

Çimi and Danja's presence was of huge importance to me. In my mind I'd carried the belief that one day nationals would put their shoulders to the church wheel in Borsh. I'd originally had no idea who they would be, or where they would come from, but their arrival was a dream fulfilled. It was important that they felt welcomed and accepted by us. In time it would also be necessary to step back and allow them the space to develop things their own way. We were reassured that they were under Paulin's leadership, and so hoped to see his dynamism and passion reflected in their approach to life and work in Borsh.

There were other encouragements that showed that our work had not been in vain. For example, shortly before vacating our base house, there was an incident that, despite being rooted in discord, bore some positive fruit. There were many early starts to our days, such as when

Joanne travelled into Saranda for an Albanian language lesson. Before catching Landi's 5.30 a.m. minibus into town she would come down to the base house for a cup of tea. There was often an early morning power cut, so we said prayers by candlelight in the winter months. We would then make our way to the top of the path and wait for Landi's bus to arrive. On the day in question, as we were waiting in the darkness, someone approached us. It took us a few moments to recognize Eqerem, because he didn't speak to us immediately. As the early morning darkness began to lift, we realized that he was holding an iron bar: he'd heard voices, and not recognizing us, feared that someone was tampering with his old Ford Transit van.

The previous evening there had been a fight with a neighbour concerning the positioning of a fence. Tempers had boiled over and someone had been hit on the head with a shovel. Now Eqerem was mindful of retaliatory action being taken. Once Joanne was on her way, I went next door with Eqerem. His wife Zuli was upset and frightened over the previous evening's fall-out, to the point of being tearful.

'What do you do when in difficult situations? Don't you lose sleep?' She posed the question during a rare exposure of personal vulnerability.

I told her candidly, 'Fear visits me every morning, but I choose not to live under its power. I pray about day-to-day situations, so would you like me to pray for you and Eqerem?'

At one time my proposal would have been considered outrageous, but now Eqerem enthusiastically said, 'Yes, yes.'

After I prayed, Zuli made a comment that betrayed her fears for the day ahead and Eqerem said, 'We have prayed to God, we should not be afraid now, he will take care of us.'

When I saw Zuli later that day, she told me that things had turned around somewhat for the good. 'Thank God,' she said.

Further evidence of spiritual awakenings came one day when I was with a handful of local men. A shepherd had roasted one of his sheep and I'd been invited to participate in the feast. One man had made a derogatory remark about how his pals were going at their food with all the finesse of a pack of hungry wolves. Amidst the laughter, Mali, the owner of the café we were sitting outside, poured me another glass of red wine. In so doing, he said something quite remarkable, his expression now serious: 'This is the blood of Christ.' The sincerity of the moment made it very poignant. Within that rough and ready setting, a sacred truth had been touched upon. We remembered Jesus in the most unlikely of circumstances.

Paulin had hit it off with some of the men from the north. The respect they had for him gave his young protégé, Çimi, a useful foothold. Each Friday afternoon, Çimi and I visited the northerners down at Flori's bar in Lower Shkalle, where they congregated at the end of the day. We usually sat outside, taking advantage of the plastic chairs and tables. Çimi fielded questions about 'The Christian Way'. I refrained from taking the lead because I wanted to promote Çimi as Borsh's 'pastor'. Sihat attended one of the early gatherings, graciously entering the territory of a man who had attacked him and badly gashed his face a year or so before, in a minor political dispute. The two men cautiously nodded towards each other; there was no confrontation. Later, as we walked along the dirt path towards home, Sihat said, 'This is how a church should be: simple, direct and honest.'

In the midst of these early encouragements, Paulin sent reinforcements down from Tirana. Altin and his wife Vjola were on the staff at The Christian Centre, working a lot with university students. A dozen of the students jumped at the chance of spending a couple of weeks by the sea, helping Çimi and Danja launch their work. I encouraged their participation, in twos and threes, in my English classes, which were still popular. One day, I was accompanied by Altin and several members of his group, including Paulin's daughter, Eva. My pupils had already enjoyed making friends with our guests from Tirana, so conversation flowed easily.

During the lesson I asked, 'What's important in life?'

Top priority for the local youngsters was their families. The students fully agreed, stating the importance of their Christian convictions. The locals enthusiastically accepted what they heard and hearts were opened. The following Sunday morning, Çimi led a Sunday morning service in a room we had hired in Ixuar, the centre of the village. Eight locals attended, including some from the English class at Roni's shop. Çimi spoke from John 15, basing his message on 'The Vine', something we had an abundance of in Borsh. After the meeting Danja served homemade cake and Coca-Cola. A village-based Christian church, under the leadership of Albanians, had been born.

Up in Vonja, the highest of the Borsh neighbourhoods, an incident encapsulated the process of handing over my work to Çimi and Danja. I was giving a lesson in the yard of Xhon and Nora's house, and had to leave for a few moments to take a friend to meet Joanne, who was making a visit nearby. When I returned, a couple of runaway lambs decided to follow me back into Xhon and Nora's yard. They caused a momentary stir when they began to nibble at my folder, and then at the plastic flowers on a little girl's sandals. As the group settled, all eyes turned to Çimi, who was having a go at teaching a little English himself. He had picked up a working knowledge of the language whilst previously working alongside American missionaries in his hometown.

Initially I felt aggrieved to see him taking over my lesson. I sat on the low wall, together with the youngsters, who were balancing their exercise books on their knees. I cared passionately about our mission in Borsh, but I would be seriously mistaken to fall into the trap of treating it as though it was my turf. Much of what we'd been hoping for, working towards and consistently remembering in our prayers was happening in front of me. Çimi was taking over. As I thought about this, my foolish pride was quietly swallowed and I realized that I should thank God for the moment. My friend Jeremy Parkes, who was visiting with his wife Joy at the time, had commented to me that day about being, 'not only educated, but enlightened on our journey.' For Çimi's birthday we gave him a special present of old-gold-coloured socks, with the motif of Wolverhampton Wanderers tastefully woven into their tops. With such a stylish addition to his wardrobe, how could he fail to impress the villagers?

When Kristin initially came to live and work in Borsh she hadn't expected to become so involved with children's work: an endeavour she fell in love with. The general condition of the schools in Borsh was poor. Stark classrooms, lack of heating in winter, missing windowpanes, foul-smelling toilets and a few well-worn textbooks, made the average school day less than stimulating. This wasn't to say that the teachers weren't committed to their pupils. On one occasion, Linda and I visited our friend Ariana at home to find her writing out individual test papers. The following day, her pupils were to have a biology exam. In the absence of school computers, photocopiers or even carbon paper, it was a manual labour of love.

Numerous children left school long before the official leaving age of 15. Dozens of teenage girls were kept home by their parents, fearful that their daughters would fall prey to the menaces of the outside world. We also knew several lads, some only 10 years old, who were sent up into the mountain each morning to tend goats.

Imagine then, when a well-educated young foreign woman arrived and started to spend time with some of the village children. Their feeling of self-worth was immediately lifted when Kristin remembered their names and took a personal interest in them. She talked of God's love for them, and with that realization, came hope and inspiration for daily life. Lessons about a way of life that focused on spiritual light, forgiveness and contentment – even in difficult times – were a revelation to young ears. No doubt some of those youngsters would leave Borsh and make a life elsewhere; others would remain. Whatever lay ahead, their childhood memories would contain an image of Kristin sitting alongside them, on a grassy bank in Kriz, or on the steps of a former prison guard's residence in Shkalle.

It was heart-wrenching for Kristin to leave Borsh behind, but when it happened, she did so for a positive reason. She met Steve, a visiting team member in 1999. They announced their engagement in the summer of 2001 and, after getting married in October the same year, lived in England for a short while before moving on to Germany.

For months after she'd left, her young friends came running up to ask, 'Where's Kristin? Please send her our love.'

* * *

Running was a pursuit that kept me physically and mentally strong. It was a discipline that made me groan when I got up at dawn to pull on my running shoes every other morning. To begin with, the sight of me running for pleasure, rain or shine, provided incredulous comment. For years I ran alone, except for one day, when a pig jogged with me for half a mile.

Every direction I ran involved the climbing of a hill. As I panted for breath on the sharp gradients, I rarely had a coherent thought pattern. However, I always felt my head was clearer at the end of a run, which I always timed, and tried to improve upon. After a while the shepherds began responding to my greetings as I ran by; less pleased to see me were the goats in their charge. They invariably occupied the full width of the road, as they dawdled behind the shepherd on their way up to the mountains. If they had to break formation, I would know about it: they gave me some very dirty looks.

Dogs were of greater concern. The concept of keeping canines for domestic pleasure hadn't yet arrived in Borsh. As if to prove the point, I'd had several pairs of trousers shredded by ill-tempered dogs. Should the owner be about at the time, I'd usually receive a muttered apology, before having the wound dabbed with *raki*. Fortunately, although snarling, aggressive dogs often rushed out at me when I entered their respective territories, I was never bitten whilst running. I always ran with a couple of stones in my hands; usually a warning shot was enough to send them packing.

Not wanting to draw attention to myself, I made sure that I did not run through the centre of the village. At the heart of it was a grocery shop owned by Merçez and Hamida, the parents of Diku. At 14 years old, Diku was a shy, overweight lad who was often mimicked by others. Even one of his former teachers would mockingly puff her cheeks out and exaggerate a waddle at the mention of his name. Maybe the shop's stock of confectionery – western chocolate bars included – played a major part in Diku's waistline. Temptation grew when he helped out in the shop during the long summer holiday. Spurred on by his sombre father, Diku started   running in order to lose weight.

The school yard was situated just a few yards behind the shop, so all he needed to do was walk across the carpet of broken bottles, discarded tin cans and other items of household waste to reach it. He ran thirty times around the concrete patch, an area a little larger than a tennis court. I'd first noticed him doing this when I walked past the school one morning. I enjoyed the fact that my own early exercise routine was an exclusively individual pursuit; running with somebody else might spoil things. As I somewhat reluctantly thought about suggesting to Diku that we ran together, I felt prompted to pray. Looking back, it was an obvious proposal to make, but the idea of running together hadn't sprung to mind immediately. My prayer was that I would become less selfish and that I would open my mind to the possibility of allowing God to use my morning jog for a new purpose.

'Maybe we could run together?' I proposed to Diku one day.

It was obvious that there were no similar reservations on his part.

His face lit up as he said, 'Yes, I would love to.'

When I turned up at the shop on the morning of our first run, his father instructed, 'Work him as hard as you can!'

As we stepped outside, Diku said something that made me smile for the rest of the morning.

'Shall we have a Snickers chocolate bar now, or when we get back?'

In fact, we occasionally shared a Snickers after our run, but only a slice at a time; whenever we did, he pressed a banana into my hand and said, 'This is for Linda.'

The first couple of times we ran together, Diku didn't open his mouth, even on uphill stretches. When I asked him why that was, he said he thought he would get a stitch if he opened his mouth. Later that day I dug out a running magazine a friend had sent me. It contained photographs of people running open mouthed. Seeing it, he too began opening his mouth whilst running and his face became a lot less purple.

Linda and I were enjoying a visit from our friend Jill Sidwell from Bedworth at about the same time we had started running together. I mentioned to her that Diku ran in normal shoes, i.e. not trainers. This soon changed; her son Marc organized a collection in the church youth group to buy Diku a pair of decent running shoes. Matthew Cairns, a lad from the same youth group, who often posted handwritten reports on Wolves' matches to me, sent out his England football shirt for Diku. My brother Vin sent him a stopwatch. These gifts not only made him look good; our running times improved considerably.

The mimicking and mocking stopped and the inhabitants of the neighbourhoods we ran through began to shout words of encouragement. I too discovered a new found joy in running, thanks to Diku. He wanted to learn my language, so we began to exchange a few words of English along certain stretches of our route.

Just as we approached our turning point, the most difficult stretch, I would encourage him with the words, 'Come on Diku, you're a strong man.'

As we ran down the road, we faced the tallest mountain in the area, the 1,700 metre high 'Maja e Dhrise'.

This is translated, 'The Mount of the Vine'. As we regularly witnessed the first shafts of morning sunlight catching its peak, I would say in English, 'Look, the sun shines on the mountain.' Diku would then repeat the words to me.

One Saturday, we climbed the mountain together. It was generally heavy going due to the loose shale underfoot. By way of compensation, we enjoyed some incredible views on our ascent. Scores of times I'd sat at the long bunker, gazing up at the mountain we were now conquering. The reverse view gave me a thrill, even though from that lofty height the bunker was little more than a dot.

When we finally reached the summit, some five hours into the climb, a cloud descended and we were denied the view I'd been looking forward to all the way up. However, we did something that was of great significance whilst up there. We wrote the words of Psalm 121 on a piece of paper; Diku wrote it in Albanian, I in English and we left it under a large stone.

When I first lived in Borsh the words, *Parti Enver*, a tribute to the late dictator, were visible a couple of hundred yards up a hillside. Student volunteers had arranged white stones to spell out the words. Nature had since taken its toll and the slogan had subsequently faded from sight. Our little piece of paper wasn't visible from ground level and I knew that in time it, too, would disintegrate. However, I always felt moved whenever I looked up at the mountain after our climb. Dictators come and go, but these words are eternal.

I lift up my eyes to the hills –
where does my help come from?
My help comes from the LORD,
the Maker of heaven and earth.

He will not let your foot slip —
he who watches over you will not slumber;
indeed, he who watches over Israel
will neither slumber nor sleep.

The LORD watches over you —
the LORD is your shade at your right hand;
the sun will not harm you by day,
nor the moon by night.

The LORD will keep you from all harm —
he will watch over your life;
the LORD will watch over your coming and going
both now and for evermore. (Ps. 121)

10

WELCOME TO HELL

'You probably won't like what I'm going to say next,' said Gary, as we sat in a restaurant one lunchtime.

Our visit to England came at a time when we were seeking direction for what lay ahead, beyond life in Borsh. Linda and I were under no pressure to move on quickly, but we understood that a pioneering work should have a finite lifespan. Either we would remain in Borsh, with different objectives, or we should move on, assured by the knowledge that Çimi and Danja would continue the work started. For the short-term future at least, Joanne would remain living and working in the village.

My Hawaiian stuffed crust pizza had been going down well until Gary said, 'I feel that your next step is to set up camp in Saranda.'

As the senior leader at church, his words carried considerable weight. Moving to Saranda wasn't what Linda and I would have chosen for ourselves, but despite being given maximum licence to operate as we saw fit, we didn't just do our own thing. Accountability and a hand of guidance from our home church were facets of mission life that we welcomed.

Upon returning to Borsh we gave the matter prayer and careful consideration. Linda and I felt that we should comply with the Saranda suggestion. We would set up home there, but sensed that our work should be concentrated outside of the town. There are dozens of villages in the area around Saranda town and we felt that our working future was in one or two of these villages. Saranda already had at least four established Christian churches, so we felt that to join and support one of them was preferable to creating yet another. Before leaving Borsh permanently, I went on scouting trips to several villages where we sensed that there was a need and the potential to develop a work.

One of the villages was Shenvasil, about an hour's bus ride in the Saranda direction. It was a village I'd travelled through hundreds of times, but rarely set foot in. Its name, translated 'St Basil', had been re-installed after being called Perparim or 'Progress' in the days of totalitarian rule. Progress wasn't a word that you'd naturally associate with the village. It was still a one horse or should I say one donkey town. Two taps on a wall in the stony village centre provided water for the three-storey apartment blocks nearby. The village square had two focal points: a single mature tree with a low wall around it, on which the men would sit and talk, and a simple war memorial. On a whitewashed wall just a few feet away, someone had scrawled graffiti. Unusually, it was written in English, 'Welcome to Hell'.

The Second World War had left a particularly ugly scar on the area. On a hot summer's day in August 1944, thirty-seven villagers were executed by Nazi machine-guns after digging a trench just outside the village centre. They had literally dug their own graves, in retaliation for a German casualty. A lone cedar dwarfs the nearby olive trees, marking the site of the massacre.

In more recent times, the village was infamous for its now derelict prison. Incarcerated there was a combination of common and political prisoners. It was to the prison I headed, after getting off the bus just before 8 a.m., one autumn morning. As I stood looking through the gates, I reflected on a story my friend, Dr Skënder from Saranda, had once told me. When the wind of freedom started blowing across Eastern Europe in the late 1980s and early 1990s, word reached the prisoners that times outside were changing. They revolted, causing the guards to react with force. A stalemate followed, as both sides refused to back out of the confrontation. A go-between was required; someone who could cope under pressure and who was respected.

Dr Skënder had worked in the area for several years as a GP. He was called upon to act as the negotiator. When he arrived at the prison, tempers were frayed and the patience of the authorities was running out. As the deadline for restoration of order passed, the prison guards cocked their guns in preparation to start shooting. Several warning shots were discharged into the air and then the guns were aimed at the rebellious prisoners standing before them. At that point, Skënder stepped forward out of the ranks of the prisoners he had been trying to calm. He shouted to the guards, 'If you are going to start killing people, you should kill me first.' Skënder's words quelled the storm. The prison governor allocated more negotiating time and it was used profitably. In the end, the political prisoners were allowed to go free and the common criminals were re-allocated to prisons across the country. The crisis had passed.

In the now overgrown yard, a stray chicken pecked about, looking for something interesting for breakfast. An elderly man approached me, wearing a flat cap and several layers of clothes beneath his dark jacket. I greeted him and he responded with a nod of his head and a slightly reticent handshake. Foreigners in his village were not an everyday occurrence.

'Who are you, where are you from?' he asked.

When I told him, a moment's silence followed.

He looked at me, clearly weighing me up.

'Would you like to come back to my house for coffee?' he said.

He had warmed to the news that I was English and we again shook hands on exchanging names.

Marku's home was just a few yards away from the old prison. He had been out to take their cow down to the large expanse of shrubby hillside slopes where it could wander freely. After taking my muddy boots off at the end of their path, which led to three whitewashed stone steps, I lowered my head to enter their home. The doorway was both low and narrow. Inside was Katerina, Marku's wife. She was dressed in the customary black and was wearing a matching headscarf. She too shook my hand and then looked quizzically towards her husband.

'He's English, I saw him by the prison and I asked him to come back for coffee,' he told her.

Marku's explanation omitted a detail she wanted to know. 'Does he speak Albanian?'

'Yes,' he said. 'He's been living in Borsh for seven years.'

Although I hadn't met this couple before, they would have heard about foreigners living in Borsh. Their warmth towards me suggested that what they'd heard about us was positive. Marku enjoyed telling me about an English soldier who'd stayed at his house one night at the end of the Second World War, as fierce fighting raged in the valley near to their home. Colour photographs of their children – all grown up and living in Greece – were mounted on the chimney breast and pointed to by Katerina as she painted thumbnail sketches of their lives. They asked me the nature of our work in Borsh and I briefly explained why I had come to live and work in Albania.

I felt prompted to pray for them and asked if I might do so. They welcomed this wholeheartedly, saying that they had a firm belief in God. The village had at one time been Orthodox and had now returned to its religious roots. Katerina requested specific prayer for her health, as she was feeling frail. After the prayer, which ended with an enthusiastic 'Amen', Katerina went into a back room. She returned holding a twenty euro note and pressed it into my hand.

'This is for the church in Borsh,' she said, much to my amazement.

Their home was humble, and by appearances, their lifestyle was a modest one; twenty euros would have been a sizeable sum to them. I instinctively found myself saying, 'No, no, I cannot accept this.'

To be offered money surprised me, to say the least. I was considered by many to be a wealthy westerner.

Katerina was insistent. 'Take it, please.'

My protests weren't going to wash as she stood over me, gently smiling. She then said something that made me realize that it was my duty to do so.

'This gives me great pleasure, because it is for God's church.'

That day Katerina taught me something I hope I will never forget. Her words had a profound impact on me. They weren't based on giving out of a sense of obligation or sympathy. She was seizing an opportunity to invest in the work of God's kingdom, an action born out of a genuine desire to give, to the point of it being sacrificial. Katerina had demonstrated the gulf between making an offering out of duty and doing so with a glad, willing spirit. I'd rarely, if ever, actively looked for opportunities to invest in the way she had.

When I saw Çimi the following day, I told him about Katerina and Marku. Çimi said that he and Danja had ordered some plastic chairs for our church meeting room. He had ordered them from Nazmi, without knowing where the money was coming from. They cost twenty euros.

With the passage of time, I visited Marku and Katerina's home on several more occasions. Two of my visits were made in the company of Skënder. He was treated like a long lost cousin by several of the people we met in the village, but the encounter with Marku and Katerina was particularly memorable. During our first informal visit, Marku produced an old Bible, which Skënder found interesting. When we called in on them again, Skënder presented the couple with a more up-to-date version, one that would be more readable. It was a gift from the Baptist Church in Saranda, which he was now leading. He read some words aloud; Katerina and Marku were absorbed.

In the corner of the room a news programme was broadcasting pictures from the Hubble space telescope on an old television set. Images of outer space, as it looked thirteen billion light years ago, were being transmitted. No one else was paying attention, but the paradox of the moment didn't escape me. A sample of the outside world's incredible technology had come to a home still without an internal water supply. By now, Skënder had lit a cigarette from one of the glowing embers in the fireplace. He was reading some words to Marku and Katerina from their new Bible: 'Get wisdom, get understanding; do not forget my words or swerve from them' (Prov. 4:5). In my eyes, this exchange was even more profound than the remarkable pictures on the television screen.

By setting up home in Saranda, Linda and I contributed to the nationwide trend of urbanization. Unlike others, our grounds for doing so were not based in economics. When the crunch came, I felt philosophical about moving on. In Borsh I'd lived through the most colourful days of my life so far, but there were few sentimental attachments from which to cut myself free. I had felt convicted to go and live there. That period of life had been special because of the presence of God's grace. To have remained there beyond our allotted time would have been unproductive and our effectiveness would have dwindled. Remaining tuned in to God's directions was of paramount importance, so leaving Borsh, when viewed in those terms, was simply the next step forward.

The spacious apartment we'd found to live in was thanks to a paediatrician who lived in the same neighbourhood of Saranda. Dr Tiri, who had been a friend for several years, made the initial contact with our landlords. The cost of living in Saranda was significantly higher, so his involvement was welcome in securing a fair contract. It was a new apartment, completed to a relatively high standard. One of its most attractive features was its hillside location. The views over the town and out to sea towards Corfu, where we enjoyed watching the ferries travelling to and from Italy, were absorbing. I likened it to looking out over a working man's Monte Carlo.

To begin with, our water supply was problematic. Few homes enjoyed the convenience of a constant water supply, so most properties, ours included, had large water tanks on their roofs. When the water came on twice a day the tanks filled up, providing the electricity supply was working to operate the pumps. In order to check our tank, I had to make my way up on to the roof via a wobbly homemade wooden ladder. No doubt it was an amusing spectacle to observe, especially if my faltering climb was made on a windy morning when all I was wearing was a dressing gown. Eventually, an improved water supply negated the need for such manoeuvres, but not before the ladder gave way beneath me and I came crashing down to earth with a bang.

Upon moving to Saranda, we knew, in principle, what the next phase of our mission would involve. Amongst other things, we felt drawn towards a church work in the nearby village of Çukë. The gypsy community there lived in poverty, but had a champion in Bedro, a middle-aged Christian woman who belonged to one of the Saranda churches. We hoped to encourage and support her work, an ambition we were to fulfil. If our work alongside Bedro came about by design, our unrelated chance meetings with Veli and Didi presented us with opportunities to rise to different challenges.

There was nothing remarkable about my first meeting with Didi, on a hot summer afternoon. At the bottom of the steep track that connects our neighbourhood with a main road, she approached me. Didi was a forlorn-looking little girl. Her hair, mousy blonde, was lank and unkempt. She was wearing a dirty T-shirt and shorts, and the purple plastic sandals on her feet were splitting. She wanted to know what time it was, and then asked me if I would like to buy some of the bay leaves she produced from a bag on her back. I had no money on me, so gave her my apologies. I promised to buy some should we meet again.

Our second meeting came a few weeks later, on a street in the town centre. This time I had money on my person.

'How much are they?' I enquired, as she apologetically held out a handful of leaves.

'Ten lek,' she replied.

This was the equivalent of five pence. We shook hands as I said, 'We will meet again,' a comment that brought the hint of a smile to her lips.

A month or so of high summer temperatures passed before our next meeting. I was in the company of some guests from St Paul's Church, Dudley. We were standing in a Saranda street when Didi appeared. She was wearing the same clothes and shoes as on our two previous meetings. She approached, but stopped short of drawing close. She stood, looking at us, a few steps away. After a few minutes she reached out to Kerry, one of the group. No words were exchanged; she simply threw her arms around Kerry's waist and hugged her. After a few moments she wandered off, the little bag still on her back.

I began making enquiries about her. Where did she live? What of her family? She had only told me her name, age and that she didn't have a mother. She was vague about her father and equally so about where she lived. Surely somebody knew something, so I began asking people who worked in the areas where I regularly saw her hanging about.

One of those locations was the street in which the town moneychangers traded. A couple of dozen men did this for a living, waving big wads of notes towards likely looking customers. The Albanian currency wasn't obtainable outside the country, so the moneychangers converted dollars or euros into lek. Opposite where they stood was the town's taxi rank. I had also seen her near to the biggest hotel in town. Day-trippers from Corfu visited an interesting third-century archaeological site at Butrint, twenty minutes outside of Saranda and were often taken to the hotel for refreshments afterwards. Didi made a little money out of the tourists as they got on or off their coaches. All those I asked had seen her regularly, but knew nothing of her home circumstances.

Skënder's wife, Liri, told me that she'd discovered where Didi lived and agreed to accompany me there.

One morning in late summer we made our way to the house, feeling apprehensive. Liri had heard mixed reports and warned me that we should be careful about getting involved. The single-storey dwelling was by the side of a road still under construction. We picked our way through the thick mud and ascended the six wooden steps that led to the entrance of the house. The ramshackle construction was made from beaten out olive-oil tins, pieces of wood, such as old doors, corrugated iron and glass. A woman came to the door, holding a young child in her arms. Solemn at first, her expression relaxed into a smile when she realized Liri and I were coming as friends.

I explained that I had met Didi several times in the street and had promised that one day I would go and meet her family. The woman told us her name was Anna. She was a half-sister of Didi's, 25 years old and had five children. She was vague about Didi's mother, but told us that Didi's father was called Hal. He was not at home, neither was Didi. Anna said we were welcome to call again and I said that next time I would take Linda with me. Liri's involvement ended after that first visit, but her role had been crucial in making the all-important first contact at Didi's home. A lone foreigner knocking on their door may have carried with it an element of threat, but Liri's presence eradicated that.

Our attitude towards Didi's family was important. Although I felt anxious about her situation, I knew I should not assume the role of someone there to police things. That authority had not been given to me. Our approach would, I hoped, be as transparent as possible. Our desire was to form a friendship with Didi and, if possible, with her family.

When Linda and I met with Hal a few days later, we were given a polite welcome. Anna made us Turkish coffee and we were encouraged to make ourselves at home. Hal's thin, unshaven face was heavily lined with wrinkles. He had a good mop of dark, unkempt hair and heavy eyes with no spark. He wore long underpants, tucked into his socks; a badly stained shirt collar was visible under a dirty jumper. Didi's 7-year-old brother clearly had the affection of his father. Every time Hal turned his face towards him a smile flickered across his lips. This was contrasted in his approach towards Didi, who had been crying prior to our arrival. When her name was mentioned he didn't even look her way, he was very cold towards her.

Linda and I started to make visits at least once a week. The next time we called, after a couple of prompts, Hal told us that Anna had gone, taking her children with her. We had taken a whiteboard and pens with us and Didi and her brother enjoyed playing with them. Hal chain-smoked throughout our visit. He made us coffee, placing the small gas burner on a wooden chair in front of him. Because he talked with a thick northern accent, it was difficult to understand much of what Hal said, but he clearly enjoyed having someone to talk to. He occasionally stopped to take an interest in what his son was doing, but not so with Didi.

As autumn passed into winter, Saturday morning visits to Hal's home became a regular part of our schedule. We took groceries with us, such as pasta, rice, coffee, sugar and chocolate for the children. As we'd discouraged Didi from hanging about on the streets, we felt that any loss of revenue on her part would be compensated for by our gift of groceries.

Establishing the bottom line in Didi's situation was almost impossible. What we were able to gather, though, told us that we had stumbled across a problem. For instance, Didi was unable to read or write, so it was clear that her schooling was severely lacking. When other children of her age were attending school she was spending time on the town's streets, looking to make money. It was difficult to determine whether she did this under duress from her father or not. Whenever I made spontaneous visits to their home, Hal said that she was out somewhere, but never knew specifically where, even after dark.

Our concerns were deepened by comments made by people who knew we were taking an interest in her. A waiter from a restaurant near to one of her favourite haunts told me that during the previous evening he had seen her standing alone outside his home. He offered her bread, which she accepted and then ran off into the darkness. Taxi drivers, a retired teacher and the occasional shopkeeper, all of whom had seen me talking to her in the street, remarked that she was in danger. She seemed to be a prime target for criminals involved in the child sex trade. Seemingly without the protective cover of parents or guardians, she could quietly be snatched off the street without causing a stir. One man told me that she was a likely candidate to be transported to a location outside of Albania to be used as a child prostitute. Many people saw the situation she was in, but nobody was actively involved in lifting her out of the trap.

In some other parts of the world, Didi's situation would have come to the attention of statutory care agencies, but for her this facility didn't appear to exist. Linda and I wanted to improve things for her from a position of trust within the family circle. This could be difficult, but we felt we had to try. We had the idea of finding and appointing a paid, part-time guardian; preferably someone with teaching experience. She would take Didi under her wing and give her some guidance in life. As we were in the process of finding such a person, a task made more difficult because of Hal's evidently poor social standing, events took a turn for the worse. Problems at home meant that Didi sometimes chose to spend entire nights out. In the absence of relatives or close friends, her disappearances were worrying.

The first time I found Didi after such a night, she was standing on a street corner. Nearby was the regular crowd, of up to a hundred and fifty strong, waiting to be hired in their ones and twos for a day's casual labour. Not many moments after we'd begun speaking, Hal arrived on the scene. A few words were exchanged and I volunteered to take everyone home in our vehicle. As we walked up the wooden steps to go inside their home, Didi held one of my hands tightly.

She refused to answer his questions as to where she'd been the previous night. When he left the room she began to cry, and said fearfully, 'He'll hit me after you've gone.' I remained with them long enough for them to begin conversing with each other. She was sitting closely to me and as I rubbed her back reassuringly, I could feel her ribs, even through her dirty blue coat. When I called back later that day, Hal was calm and courteous, but Didi was out yet again.

More cold nights out followed. One morning I found Didi rummaging through a roadside heap of domestic rubbish. She fingered through a pile of discarded playing cards as she said that her father wasn't always honest with me and that she didn't want to return home. By now Linda and I had secured a definite offer of help from a respected former teacher, a middle-aged widow, called Vera Diamond. We believed her to be a person of integrity, following the many positive references received about her from, among others, fellow members of the church she attended in town.

Vera accompanied us on a visit to Hal's home one afternoon. She was humble in her approach, acknowledging Hal's challenges in bringing up Didi single-handedly, and then gently offering non-intrusive help. As an employee of the town's children's home, Vera would welcome Didi to visit her at her place of work several times a week for friendly but structured tuition. Although Hal made all the right noises, we came away from our discussion with him feeling less than convinced of his complete approval. His endorsement of our proposal was essential if it was to succeed.

Our attempts to get Didi to visit Vera came to nothing. We suspected that Hal, despite repeatedly stating otherwise, resented outside support. By implication, he would be seen to be an inadequate father. Frustrated as we were, we had to remind ourselves that we were guests in Albania, so carried no legal jurisdiction with us. Our efforts were based on goodwill and determination. Getting legal backing to pull Didi out of the hole she was in would have compromised our relationship with her father. Ultimately, something would have to give. We would not give up on her.

After being out for four consecutive nights, I found her in a side street in the town. Darkness had already fallen and another bitterly cold night lay ahead. She pleaded with me not to take her back home.

'Where do we go then?' I asked.

Our first port of call was to a couple I knew had had contact with Didi in the past. This time she was not treated sympathetically.

'She's a parasite,' I was told, and we left feeling deflated.

'Isn't he a bad-tempered man?' Didi said, as we walked along the road, her small, cold hand in mine.

I didn't want to take her to our home; I had to guard against opening ourselves up to being accused of kidnapping her, or something even worse than that. 'Where do we go, Didi?'

Far from being miserable, her mood, superficially, was remarkably light.

'I'll sleep up in the mountain,' she replied.

She laughed when I said she might get eaten by wolves and came up with another suggestion.

'I'll sleep in your car,' she said with a cheeky grin.

I told her that it wasn't a good idea, conscious of what others would think of a lone western male talking at length to a small girl in the street at night time. There was nowhere obvious to take her; both the police and the local authority were an unknown quantity to me in such matters.

'Why don't we go to the children's home?' I suggested.

This, I felt, was our best option. It took a while to convince Didi before she finally agreed to go inside, in part, as a personal favour to me.

The night carer, Nora, made a telephone call to obtain permission for Didi to spend the night there. Once authorization had been given, we were told to make our way up the concrete stairs to the television room. Upon entering, all those present stood up – a sign of respect for a visiting adult. They sat down again, on the slightly battered armchairs, arranged in rows in front of the television. Although the room had few home comforts, it had a friendly feel to it. Didi had asked if I'd stay with her for a while, so I made myself comfortable on one of the chairs and reached for my glasses, so I could watch the film.

The dozen or so girls in the room, aged from 8 to 16, closely monitored me.

'I need these to see the television,' I stated, pointing to the glasses.

Many of them smiled and the ice was broken. All eyes returned to the television set. Presently, one of the girls stood up and carefully cradled the cat that had been sitting on her lap, wrapped in an old shirt. She gently placed it onto Didi's lap and said softly, 'Hello, Didi.'

It was a lovely gesture of welcome. Evidently the girls from the children's home already knew Didi but previous attempts to get her in had ended in failure. A few more minutes passed and Didi looked up at me, her nose less red from the cold night air.

'I think I'll be all right now, but will you come and see me early tomorrow morning?' she whispered.

I agreed to her request and after squeezing one of her hands reassuringly, bid her and the rest of the girls goodnight.

The following morning I made my way up to the television room once more. A little girl, wearing glasses attached to a cord, was straightening the chairs.

'Good morning, how are you?' I asked.

She continued with the task in hand and said confidently, in English, 'I'm fine.'

A Tarzan cartoon was on the television and a boy came to watch it with me. After a few moments, Didi walked in with two other girls. She was wearing clean clothes and her hair, still wet from showering, was kept from falling over her ears by coloured slides. She looked bright eyed and cheerful.

'How did you sleep?' I asked.

'Really well, I have a bed in a room with two other girls,' she beamed.

She was much more relaxed than she had been the previous evening. After a few moments she headed towards the door with her two friends.

'Breakfast is ready,' she said.

There was no question of her wanting to leave with me, much to my relief.

The following day I met with Hal at his home. I wanted him to hear from me that Didi was in the children's home. He didn't react to the news, making me the usual cup of coffee, smoking two or three cigarettes and then wishing me well for the rest of the day. I called for Linda and we went to the home to see the Director and her deputy. Although the meeting was formal, the content of what they had to say was particularly pleasing.

'Here she will be given a home and a family. She is welcome to stay as long as she likes.'

During the following weeks the road ahead was far from smooth. Hal snatched Didi back at least twice, breaking her young heart in the process. The second time she was returned to the children's home it was by the police, who used force. By now, a local authority worker and a friend of ours, Elida, who had taken a keen interest in Didi's situation, were on board, helping to secure her position. This didn't come without a price.

At 7 a.m., the day after the police recovered Didi, there was a knock at our front door. It was Hal. I hadn't been back home long, following my usual morning jog, so I answered the door still wet from my shower and wearing a dressing gown. Hal's eyes had the look of menace about them, as he delivered an ultimatum. If I didn't arrange for the immediate discharge of Didi, he would get a gun and I would have an accident on the road one day. With that, our short exchange came to a close. As I dressed, I thought about what Hal had said: it was a threat I had to take seriously. I had no regrets whatsoever about taking Didi to a place of sanctuary. Taking action to have her discharged from the children's home wasn't something I was prepared to do.

Linda and I were of the same mind. However, I had to consider our safety, as well as Joanne's. By this time she had also come to live in a Saranda apartment, though her work remained village focused, particularly in Borsh. I took advice from people who understood the lie of the land. How serious a threat was hanging over us? Joanne had never had direct contact with Hal, so she would not be in any danger. It would also be unlikely that Linda would be included in any act of misguided vengeance. For my part, I was told that I had nothing to lose sleep over. Had we suspected that there was an element of genuine risk, we would have slipped out of town until the situation had cooled down.

To date, my relationship with Hal remains a casualty of Didi's story. He does not share our relief in seeing his daughter established at Saranda's children's home. When Didi began living there, her life changed, but so did other things too. The way that Hal had been able to walk unchallenged into the yard, had highlighted a vacuum in security. Soon afterwards, a lock was attached to the gate and a twenty-four hour security guard service was introduced.

One day I came across the place I suspected Didi had been sleeping, prior to her rescue. At the bottom of a stairwell, in a town centre apartment block was a cardboard box, big enough for a little girl. Now she was free from that uncertain world, free from the imminent threat of being a victim of the trade in human trafficking.

Didi's life continues to be transformed. Her eyes, free of the dark shadows, sparkle whenever she sees us. For the majority of Albanian children – and for millions of others across the world – school, regular meals, hygiene, decent clothing and general safety are normal ingredients of life. Now Didi can enjoy these privileges. Vera Diamond continues to keep a protective eye on her, and she is often at church, where she joins the other girls from the children's home for Sunday meetings. Our hearts warm as we watch her singing her heart out, albeit out of tune.

Just as Didi came into our lives unexpectedly, the same can be said of Veli, a man more than sixty years her senior. Tragically for him, at just 13 years of age, he was sentenced to a twenty-five-year period of internment in a political prison. In Didi's case, we had been given an opportunity to help her set foot on a better road in life. For Veli, no such escape route had existed. In the closing chapters of his life, we had a chance to extend a hand of compassion and friendship in his direction.

Our first meeting came about as a consequence of a bulldozer driver's carelessness. He had fractured a water pipe, rendering the block of flats a few yards from our home, waterless. One morning as I was walking down the hill, I met a bent old woman, dressed in black from head to toe. She was coming the other way, struggling with four full water containers. She made no protest when I took them from her and asked her to lead the way home. She wheezed and panted her way to the third floor of the flats, then cupped a hand behind my neck to pull me down towards her so that she could kiss me. Her wrinkled face was soft to the touch.

Later that same day, I took more water and was asked to take a seat in the kitchen and lounge area. I'd been welcomed in by Veli, the old lady's son-in-law. He had a shock of white hair, dark eyes, sunken cheeks and two silver stumps that served as teeth. With the exception of a large stuffed toy leopard that was sprawled across the top of the fridge-freezer, their flat was furnished with familiar uniformity. Veli put an open pack of cigarettes on the glass-topped coffee table and encouraged me to take one. The old lady busied herself making Turkish coffee.

'Thank you, but I don't smoke,' I told him.

'Good for you,' he said with a phlegmy cough, before telling me that he'd been smoking since he was 7 years old.

He proudly told me that his origins were in Vlore, where his family had once enjoyed a comfortable lifestyle. His father had been a wealthy landowner and that made him an enemy of the emerging 'Worker's Party'. In 1944, the family lost everything. They didn't go down without a fight however, as the entire family, including 13-year-old Veli, found itself on the wrong side of the political divide. As my coffee was placed on the table by his mother-in-law, Veli led me into his bedroom. He pointed towards a photograph on the wall above his bed. It was an old black and white portrait of his deceased brother, executed when he was 20 years old.

Veli had served nearly twenty-five years of hard labour in political prison. His working day, digging and tunnelling rock, was usually spent up to his waist in water. The food ration consisted of a watery soup: barely enough to keep him alive. His face lit up on hearing that I was British.

'The British Prime Minister, Tony Blair, is someone I have great respect for,' he said.

Veli went on to explain that he saw Tony Blair as a liberator.

'I know what it's like to live under an evil regime. Every time I see Tony Blair's face on my television set, I kiss the screen,' he said. 'I love the British people and want to tell them that.'

We became great friends. His wife, daughter and two sons were living in Greece, where they had found work. In their absence, due to Veli's chronic breathing and heart problems, I gradually became a personal attendant to him.

If our mission wasn't in existence to help the likes of Veli, then what was its purpose? This thought was one I reminded myself of on the days when I was running numerous errands for him. These tasks gave me an insight into some of the difficulties and hardships faced by Albanian pensioners. Veli's own monthly allowance was the equivalent of £45. More than half of it was immediately swallowed up by the monthly medication he needed to take. On pension days I accompanied him about town. Our usual route took in the butchers for frozen chicken legs, a shop that sold cut-price cigarettes and a café where Veli enjoyed a hot chocolate. Obtaining medication took many hours of waiting around in the town's hospital for doctors, who had to comply with a system top heavy with bureaucracy.

Whenever his condition deteriorated, he would spend long periods in hospital. On one occasion I took him to be admitted. After a brief examination, the duty doctor said that he wasn't fit to go back home. Veli reluctantly accepted a pair of pyjamas in exchange for his trousers and a written receipt. The rest of his clothes stayed on, beneath his pyjamas. In the absence of a hospital lift, he held my hand as we negotiated several flights of steps. A nurse pointed to a twin-bedded room and Veli bristled when he saw that one of the beds was already occupied. He wanted a room to himself and, such was his strength of character, despite his lack of breath, succeeded in getting it.

I soon found myself helping to carry the other patient's bedclothes to an alternative room, further down the corridor. After repositioning and then helping Veli make up his bed, I was given more instructions.

'Take some of the sauce out of this stew I brought with me and pour it over that top door hinge.'

I opened the plastic margarine tub and spooned out enough to pour over the offending hinge. Sure enough, the squeak he'd noticed was eradicated, much to his satisfaction.

I visited him most days and became friendly with the poorly paid but well-meaning doctors and nurses. After watching me share a word of prayer with Veli, some of the other patients began to ask me to pray for them. It occurred to me that, despite being an unknown concept in these parts, a hospital chaplaincy would go down well. The lack of equipment was obvious, even to my unqualified eyes.

When Veli needed oxygen, he had to take his turn with three other patients who also had access to the only bottle on the ward. He decided he wanted his own oxygen bottle, specifically for use back home. He was to be discharged from hospital a few days later. Despite being told officially that it was out of the question, because they weren't available, he obtained one. What I will politely refer to as 'private enterprise' won through. Our concerns were that, as a heavy smoker, there was a risk of him blowing himself up and taking the rest of the block of flats with him. Nonetheless, he got his own way and made use of someone who had access to an oxygen supply.

Communist Albania had boasted of its healthcare system, quoting hugely improved life expectancy figures, thanks to its efficiency. Figures published said that in 1938 the average life expectancy in Albania was only 38 years. In 1950 it rose to 53 years and in 1976 to 69 years. Now, Albania is a democratic country, but the legacies of the old institutions remain. My insight into the current 'system' is that if it ever really was a well-run machine, it has now become rusty and uncoordinated.

Veli's chronic health problems could have been partially alleviated by what Joanne called 'a basic nursing procedure'. Fluid puffed his feet and ankles up and it would have helped to sleep with his feet raised. However, it didn't happen, either in hospital or at home. As with many old people, he had a belief in popular medicine.

One day I called to see him before moving on to Çukë, an out of town neighbourhood that bordered marshland. When I told him where I was going, his eyes lit up.

He announced, with typical assertiveness, 'I want you to get me something from Çukë that will take the swelling from my feet. Catch me four leeches.'

A mental picture flashed through my mind in which I was standing up to my knees in water with an open jam jar in one of my hands.

Before I said anything, his mother-in-law, not wanting to miss out said, 'I'd like one too.'

Veli's eyes returned to mine, 'You'd better make it five.'

I always tried to do my best for him, but on this occasion I'd met my Waterloo. I made up for it with some of his favourite fruit, a bag of locally grown pomegranates.

He is a cantankerous old boy who mutters and swears under his breath at the least provocation. On a visit to the barber's shop one morning, he found it most unreasonable that the customer waiting in front of him didn't want to give up his place in the queue.

'You still have a strong spirit,' I often counter, a remark that is usually greeted by a mischievous wink.

We have built a close friendship and for such a tough old man, he surprises me with his affection. He regularly kisses me on the cheeks and tells me, 'I love you like a son and Linda like a daughter.'

* * *

Linda and I took our time in deciding which church to attend. Rightly or wrongly, we regarded our prospective church life as an extension of our working life. With the emphasis on encouraging local leaders, our choice of church was based on establishing where we would be most useful, rather than where we had the best time. That wasn't to say that you couldn't have fun whilst serving others; it was a case of going to wherever duty called the loudest.

We had been living in Saranda for a few months and had become *au fait* with ferry times, sailing to and from Corfu. We had also built up a good rapport with the providers of essential services in Corfu. People travelling through, usually from the Christian community in Albania, began to make contact with us, to pick our brains for information.

One day I met some Americans off a boat and put them on a bus to their next destination. One of them, who I'd shown to a café toilet, turned to me.

'I don't know if you believe in this sort of thing or not, but I feel there is something I have to say to you. You are surrounded by many doors at present and are thinking about which one to open. Take your time, there's no rush, because it will become obvious as to which doorway you should enter.'

With that, he was on his way. He knew nothing of our personal circumstances.

Linda and I decided to attend a church started in 1995 by a Romanian called Pal. After he had moved on to begin a work elsewhere, Indian-born Magdalena, a convert from Hinduism, led the church. It was under her dynamic leadership that Nedo, whose husband worked for the Albanian Navy, Bedro, who'd pioneered the work with the gypsies and Vera Diamond all came to the fore. When Magdalena moved to Tirana, it was these three women who took over the reins of leading The Triumphant Life Church.

'My son spends too much time watching television and not enough time doing his homework,' Bedro said one day as we travelled in our car together.

We were going to spend an hour or so with the people from an ostracized community. Many things about Bedro's life are average: her husband is an electrician, they live in a town centre apartment with son Klajdi and have a married daughter in another part of Albania. It is her dedication to the gypsies of Çukë that makes her exceptional.

Within a culture where indifference to others is a sign of changing times, Bedro selflessly gives up her time to share her faith with a community of fifty people, only three of whom can read and write. They live in the poorest of housing on the edge of a village that has lost most of its inhabitants to Greece. Walking from our parked vehicle to where they live involves having to pick our way through mud and cow manure. Even so, Bedro's appearance, including her shoes, remains immaculate. I have often wondered how Albanians, women in particular, are able to keep their shoes so clean.

The church at Çukë meet in a purpose built room at the back of the home of Agron and Mirela, a couple in their mid-thirties. Their youngsters once invited me to watch a televised football match with them. The electricity supply in their neighbourhood was so low that we had to wait for the people living next door to finish using their electric cooker before the television set would work. The church meetings are inevitably rough and ready affairs; it's not uncommon for a male member of the community to wander in smoking a cigarette, look around and casually walk out again. Bedro demands order, and usually gets it, during the times when she addresses them.

Respect is given when Holy Communion is celebrated, which is usually presided over by Odeta, a teenage helper from the mother church in Saranda. Foreign visitors are enthusiastically welcomed. During clothes and food distribution times, Bedro is at the sharp end, often receiving unjustifiable criticism for the contents of gift bags. She takes it all in her stride, making house calls to offer a word of advice or to share a prayer accordingly. She never speaks badly about the people she lovingly befriends, even though they are looked down upon by almost everyone else. One day, Silvana, who gets up at 4 a.m. to go and clean the streets of Saranda, was hit by a car as she worked. Such was the contempt for Silvana and her friends that the driver did not bother to stop.

I have thought many times about the qualities that distinguish one person from the next. It isn't an original observation on my part; the Apostle Paul beat me to it by almost two thousand years. He talks in Romans about suffering, perseverance, character and hope. It's a favourite theme of mine because the people we rub shoulders with personify the first three links in the chain. This is particularly true of Albanians, who have lived through the worst of their country's totalitarian regime. The final, all-important fruit of hope is the one we see least evidence of. When we consider Bedro, doing her work with the gypsies week by week, we see hope for a better tomorrow.

Over a number of months I collected photographs that captured different events in the life of the church at Çukë. Some snaps featured children playing football or cricket. Others were photographed wiggling their hips inside gyrating hula-hoops. There were prints of a picnic attended by visitors from overseas, people singing in church accompanied by Diti on his guitar, and several close-ups of both young and old. One day I went to Çukë to mount the photographs on a wall in our meeting room. I needed to work freely away from the well-meaning but unhelpful intrusions of the children and so I locked the door behind me. At first, several of the children, some of them without shoes, hammered on the door. They were curious to know what I was up to. Eventually, something else caught their attention and they went away.

As I worked quietly, I had time to think. Over the years, I felt I'd had many more failures than successes in my efforts at evangelism. Practical expressions of love were arguably better received than the spoken ones, but it was extremely hard to quantify. Church attendance was usually considerably higher on the days when goodies were given out. Bedro, often stirred up by the fickleness of the gypsies, occasionally threw down the gauntlet.

She asked the difficult question, 'Do you come because you have a genuine spiritual hunger, or do you come only for the food and clothes we give you?'

She would later comment to us, as we drove back home, that she didn't really know where any of them stood as regards true faith in God. It was a sentiment I too could relate to regarding many friends of mine in Borsh and Saranda.

When the job was completed, I unlocked the door. As the children spilled in, closely followed by several mothers, they became excited at the sight of the display. As the others eagerly scanned the wall, looking for photographs of themselves, Mirela's gaze remained fixed on the words of Scripture that was the centrepiece to the display. Although Linda had written them out before I left home, it was only when Mirela read them aloud, for the benefit of her neighbours who couldn't read, that a penny dropped. No matter how discerning I was, or could ever aspire to be, some things, such as what is truly in a person's heart, are only for God to know.

'Listen, this is what the words say,' she said. '"I am The Good Shepherd; I know my sheep and my sheep know me."'

11

THE INVISIBLE SERVANT

I am always apprehensive when our suitcases are weighed on the scales at airport check-in counters. I haven't heard the words, 'I'm sorry your bags are overweight,' but one day the axe is bound to fall. Return journeys from England are usually made with our bags bulging. Certain items are allocated a 'five-star' tag of priority: chocolate, music CDs and a few decent books are always a must.

The books are often about British history, a subject I've developed a great fondness for. Many Albanians talk enthusiastically about the richness of British culture, so I decided to fill in some of the gaps in my knowledge. I read about the Victorian era of British history with particular interest. A heavyweight publication had given me a good background on the subject, including information about domestic service. In 1851 there were three quarters of a million servants in Britain, rising to just under one and a half million in 1891. Another purchase, with an eye-catching title and cover, was for lighter reading.

Primarily written for youngsters, it described the life of a domestic servant in the nineteenth century. As I read about the qualities of a good servant, something jumped out at me. Invisibility was listed as one of the qualities. This wasn't just applicable to a bygone age; it was true in the here and now. I realized that I was looking in fact at a personal template.

The best servants had to satisfy a set of criteria. To convince a prospective employer of his or her honesty and diligence, the applicant would be set a test. A coin was placed under a carpet in a room that was to be given a trial clean. If the coin was not found, because of a lack of thoroughness, they failed the test. If it was discovered and then pocketed, they were found to be dishonest. Only when the coin was handed over was that particular test passed; the person would then be considered both thorough and honest. Other criteria included general fitness and, preferably, an independence from commitments outside of the workplace.[1]

The requirement to be invisible was not to be taken literally of course; it was a way of saying that they should be inconspicuous. They were so well tuned in to their employer's needs that they carried out their duties, without drawing attention to themselves. It was important to complete the act of service to the required standard: personal profile counted for nothing. To others, their presence was practically unperceivable.

How did this relate to my life? I had gone to live in a land that had once been dominated by secret service spies. For decades the Albanian people had to make snap decisions about strangers. Could they be trusted or not? I knew from the beginning that my attitude towards others was of crucial importance. If this wasn't right, then how could I win people's hearts? Bearing that in mind, I devoured some sound advice on the subject from the Apostle Paul. The first church on European soil had begun in the Roman colony of Philippi, located in North Eastern Greece, probably about AD 50. Paul wrote a letter to the church containing specific instructions regarding attitude:

Do nothing out of selfish ambition or vain conceit, but in
humility consider others better than yourselves. Each of
you should look not only to your own interests, but also to
the interests of others. Your attitude should be the same as
that of Christ Jesus: Who, being in very nature God, did not
consider equality with God something to be grasped, but
made himself nothing, taking the very nature of a servant,
being made in human likeness. And being found in appearance as a man, he humbled himself and became obedient to
death – even death on a cross!

(Phil. 2:3–8)

This passage became vitally important to me. 'The servant heart' was an expression I had heard so many times
before that by now it just washed over me. As I thought
about all the implications of being a servant to the people I was living amongst, I realized how appropriate the
invisible servant theme was. It became my driving force.

In trying to take on the nature of a servant in Albania,
I realized I had to grow thicker skin. Gradually, I realized
that there were three distinct phases of this metamor-
phosis. I would need to negotiate all three if I was serious about it. The first was deciding that this was what I
wanted to become. Personal pride had to be forfeited.
The second was tougher, because it meant doing something about it. The third stage was the most difficult,
because some people began to treat me like a servant.
Volunteering to do something and getting thanked for it
was very different to being expected to do something
without thanks. Being taken advantage of sometimes left
me smarting.

'What a cheek,' I'd think.

With hindsight, it seems petty to recount times
when I was expected to run a taxi service. In both
Borsh and Saranda this happened frequently. Being

inconvenienced, for a variety of reasons, has become something of a way of life. It's been necessary for me to learn genuine patience.

The 'Invisible Servant' concept helped me immensely. No doubt, 'invisible' acts of service are sometimes accredited to others. Most of us enjoy receiving praise. However, seeing others receiving the credit for one's own actions can be a bitter pill to swallow. In my case, much of the dilemma can be attributed to an old adversary, personal pride. Following the servant example of Jesus, as Paul urged, provided me with the answer: 'Jesus made himself of no reputation.' Frequent reflection upon these words has helped me to keep things in perspective.

Sources of inspiration are a welcome discovery whatever our chosen field of endeavour happens to be. Just as we are told that multivitamins can help keep our bodies strong, I'm encouraged whenever I come across nuggets of wisdom. The ones that can be applied to everyday life have a particularly fortifying effect on me.

* * *

Jonny Wilkinson's match-winning drop goal for England in the 2003 Rugby World Cup Final provided a wonderful sporting memory. As far as personal favourites are concerned, it ranks alongside John Richards and Andy Gray scoring winning goals for Wolves at Wembley, in 1974 and 1980 respectively. There may be just a tad of old-gold and black bias in there, but I never tire of watching recordings of such glorious moments.

I'd watched the rugby game in a Cardiff hotel. Linda's daughter, Sophie, was studying at the university and we had gone for a weekend visit. Following England's triumph I became, like thousands of others, intrigued by the story behind the success. England's coach, Sir Clive Woodward, revealed that when he took over the squad, his players were far from being world class. He talked of how he identified two categories of players: energizers and energy sappers. As I understood it, he made a crucial decision to drop the energy sappers and replace them with more energizers. That way his team could be built from a pool of like-minded, positive people.

It occurred to me, that although the sporting analogy couldn't be fully applied to mission life, there were some parallels. I would like to think that I became more effective in my work as a consequence. By recognizing that discouragement, failure, being misunderstood, being taken advantage of and sometimes getting ripped off, all belonged in the energy sapper's camp, I could manage those experiences with greater understanding. We were not in the business of dropping those who made exhausting demands upon us, but we could, at least, be more adept in knowing when to wear body armour.

Energizers are a wonderful thing. Fortunately, just as we seek to energize others, there are people in my life who energize me and I thank God for them. Far from being sent out into the field and then forgotten, I have been privileged to have had consistent support and friendship back at base. Scooter smashes aside, Gary has stood shoulder to shoulder with me for the ten years of my involvement with the church's mission to Albania. If Henry Ford's adage, 'My best friend is the one who brings out the best in me' is true, then Gary's friendship is precious indeed.

Towards the end of one of his stays with us, he joined Linda and me for a walk along Saranda's new promenade. With the constant 'rat-tat-tat' of rock hammers in the background, we gazed up at the new generation of concrete constructions. Some people say with a smile that there will soon be enough new hotels in Albania to accommodate all of Europe. A few moments after passing an internet café, an Albanian woman introduced herself to us. Her sister had been widowed four years earlier when her husband, along with two friends and a 12-year-old boy, were tragically blown to pieces in a fishing boat accident.

On hearing about it, Gary had organized a collection at church that raised enough money to allow us to give a loaf of bread to each bereaved family every day for three years.

'I'd like to thank you for the help you gave my sister at a time when she faced great need, even though you didn't know her,' she said.

I was delighted that Gary was present to hear what she had to say; he was on hand to witness the result of an effort he, with the help of others, had initiated from thousands of miles away.

It was during that visit that Gary asked me to seriously consider writing this book. He had suggested it several times before, as had Linda, but I'd always resisted the idea.

When he raised it again, Gary said, 'We invariably focus on the destinations and don't give enough attention to the journeys involved in getting there. Your personal journey is one that others might like to read about.'

I agreed to pray about it. That wasn't a way of fudging the issue, I meant it.

Several weeks later, I was drinking coffee in a village café with a school headmaster I had just met.

Quite out of the blue he said, 'You should write a book about your time in my country.'

I took this to be a further confirmation that I should accept the idea to write a book. Sure enough, I eventually said, 'Yes,' and Linda went on to type out every word. This was in addition to acting as unofficial editor; no one else could tell me that some of my first drafts were a load of 'tosh' quite as nicely as she did.

When I first moved to Albania, no one really knew what to expect. Others may have accomplished more than I have, and in less time. I trust that in reading this you will understand that I have sought to give you a personal perspective, rather than write a definitive history of the country or a textbook on mission life.

Some situations have brought with them considerable heartache, but not every twist and turn of the past ten years has been recounted. Reading about the stresses and strains of others has encouraged me when faced with my own challenges. However, Abraham Lincoln said, 'Better to remain silent and be thought a fool than to speak out and remove all doubt.' There have been many occasions when in the company of Albanians that my flawed mastery of their language has prevented me from opening my mouth. When recalling Lincoln's words in such situations, I have often smiled quietly to myself. By the same token, despite my desire to be as transparent as possible, some things will remain untold.

I would like to think that along the way, I have learnt to differentiate between the spectacular and the significant. Within my experience, the two things rarely arrive in the same package. Saranda, probably like every other town in Albania, greets the arrival of a New Year with a battery of fireworks. It's as if every balcony in town becomes a launch pad for rockets, which explode spectacularly in the night sky at the stroke of midnight. After watching the final dart of colour fade away, our eyes return to ground level: it's there that the business of life continues.

In terms of mission life, it's been our experience that significant developments have only come about as a result of perseverance and mundane duty. Whilst my dramatic airlift out of Albania in 1997 was spectacular, it was far from being the most significant event in the life of our mission. By contrast, there was nothing spectacular about Pellumbi and Drita's walk to church in Borsh, one wet winter morning. They arrived soaked to the skin; a forty-five minute walk in inclement weather, along a rough road, wasn't going to stop them. They wanted to attend the meeting, presided over by Çimi; in my opinion, that moment was truly significant.

A worthwhile account of my time in Albania to date would not be complete without telling you about another significant echo from British history. It had a profound effect on me and helped shape my thinking about our work from that time onward. Linda and I were enjoying the rugged countryside of Northumbria, not far from Lindisfarne, England. We came across some works of literature that described the work of Celtic missionaries in The Dark Age. The manner in which they went about their work is something I have tried to emulate. Fourteen hundred years ago, a light began to shine in the darkness. It was the dawning of The Church in Britain.

We read that the Celtic missionaries went about their work with sensitivity and gentleness. Their intention was not to impose an alien culture on to those they befriended and lived alongside. On the contrary, they respected the views of others and acknowledged the merits of their beliefs. Ian Bradley's book, *The Celtic Way*, puts it this way: 'The Celtic church did not so much seek to bring Christ as to discover Him; not to possess Him, but to seek Him in "friend and stranger", to liberate the Christ who is already there in all His riches.'[2]

This was food for thought. If I had ever imagined that I had taken God to Albania with me, when I'd first packed my suitcase, I would have been seriously mistaken. Perhaps I'd thought that in due course I would introduce him to the people I'd gone to live among.

It is a historical fact that Albania officially denied God's existence for several decades but this did not mean that he remained a stranger to all of her citizens. As we have already considered elsewhere, many Albanians loved God to the point of dying for their faith. I came to understand, thanks to the Celtic missionaries, that my own journey of faith was being made together with my Albanian friends.

The road I have been travelling down may have contained some narrow stretches, but I've remained convinced that it's a track I was meant to be on. It has taken me a long way from England, the place I still think of as home. Despite living away for ten years, I feel more English than ever. This may, in part, be attributable to being referred to as *Anglezi* when I meet strangers. I am increasingly aware of the love I have for our family and friends. Even though our times together have been restricted, the bonds between us have somehow become stronger. This separation has been the greatest price we have had to pay over the last ten years; their acceptance and patience means a lot.

My life has been considerably enriched because of the decision I took ten years ago to truly trust God. It has felt natural to be in Albania, even though the physical surroundings and culture are very different from home. Whilst there have been many confirmations of this, one in particular sticks in my memory. Despite the brevity of our association, something Juan Coll said has remained with me. I hadn't been living in Albania long when I met Juan, a Spaniard who, at the time, was in his early twenties. He was trying to see as much of the world as possible; I sensed that it was also something of a voyage of self-discovery. Just before he made his way to Saranda Port, to embark on the next leg of his travels, I wished him well.

In response, he said to me, 'I have travelled sixty thousand kilometres and I am still lost, but in your case, you have found your place.'

* * *

Beautiful mountain scenery, daily power cuts, summer heat and cold winters will no doubt provide enduring memories of life in Albania. I am sure that images of certain people's faces and the sounds of their voices will remain in our hearts for a long time. We have been honoured to count as our friends, people who have endured the excesses of a dictatorship, the likes of which we are unlikely ever to experience. I have learnt many things from my Albanian friends, not least about strength of character, something I attribute to their remarkable capacity for endurance. I would love to think that our mission has made a positive contribution towards bringing hope: it is, after all, the fruit of character.

With that in mind, the closing words of my book will come from an Albanian. This is only fitting, since so much of my story really belongs to the Albanian people. Although Erjon is too young to remember his country's most recent era of persecution, he is no stranger to trauma. One evening his cousin was shot dead whilst at Erjon's side. Fearing that his son would meet a similar fate, Erjon's father asked me to befriend Erjon and teach him English. A working knowledge of the English language would, in his father's view, enhance his prospects.

Erjon and I became friends, reaching out to discover the love of God together. Sometimes it was difficult to teach him much because of all the food his mother served me. However, he once said something to me that signifies considerable hope for the future. One day, before the inevitable tray of refreshments arrived, Erjon learnt the word 'beautiful'. I asked him to create a sentence containing the new word. After thinking about it for a few moments, he said, 'The meaning of life is a beautiful thing.'

---

[1] Terry Deary, *The Vile Victorians* (London: Scholastic Publications Ltd, 1994).
[2] Ian Bradley, *The Celtic Way* (London: Darton, Longman & Todd Ltd, 1993).

Contact information

If you want to know more about Richard and Linda's work, please contact them in one of the following ways:

Write to: ✳

The Church Missions Office
King's Community Church
The Christian Centre
Bulkington Road
Bedworth
Warwickshire
CV12 9DG

Online: http://www.kingscc.co.uk

Phone the following number: 02476 494320

E-mails can also be sent via David Waite:
davidj.waite@btopenworld.com

✳ squelched 77 @ yahoo. com